Who was Mr Nobody?

Who was Mr Nobody?

DEBUNKING HISTORICAL MYSTERIES

ED RAYNER AND RON STAPLEY
AUTHORS OF *DEBUNKING HISTORY*

SUTTON PUBLISHING

First published in the United Kingdom in 2007 by
Sutton Publishing, an imprint of NPI Media
Cirencester Road · Chalford · Gloucestershire · GL6 8PE

© Ed Rayner and Ron Stapley, 2007

Reprinted 2007

British Library Cataloguing in Publication Data
A catalogue record for this book is available from the British
Library.

ISBN 978-0-7509-4605-8

Typeset in Melior
Typesetting and origination by
Sutton Publishing Limited.
Printed and bound in England.

To our wives:
Pamela Ann Rayner
(who died on 1 April 2005)
and
Enid Margaret Stapley

Contents

CONTENTS

Preface

History is littered with mysteries that puzzle modern observers. Some emerge from the little-known byways of the subject. Some go back to early times, and are the more baffling because they have never been unravelled, like the fate of the ancient Greek city that vanished under the sea and gave rise to the legend of Atlantis. However, this book does not deal with obscure or far-off episodes. It confines itself to the period since Tudor times, and so deals with the more modern and accessible mysteries of the past.

The ramifications of some, like the murder of the two little princes in the Tower of London at the end of the fifteenth century, rest in times long past, yet imply consequences the importance of which is still with us today. Others are more modern and have a topical, even contemporary interest, like the mysterious burning of the German Reichstag in 1933, or the unexplained sinking of the Russian submarine *Kursk* in the Barents Sea in August 2000.

The mysteries have been grouped into six loose categories. The first, 'Dead or Alive?', deals with the fate of kings and other leaders sometimes suspected of having come to a sticky end. The second, 'Mysterious Identities', examines other, often quite famous, historical figures, whose stories suppose some kind of mystery. Then come explorations of 'Murder and Mayhem', 'Plots and Intrigues', and 'Military, Naval and Air Mysteries'. The final part, 'Mysteries, Secrets and Disappearances', looks at historical puzzles that have never been solved, or for which there is no commonly agreed explanation.

The exploration of each mystery contains descriptive as well as analytical material for the benefit of those unfamiliar with the subject-matter under discussion. We ask forgiveness for any item that the reader believes should have been included, but which we, because of shortage of space or because of our own ignorance, have managed to overlook.

Ed Rayner and Ron Stapley

1

Dead or Alive?

WHO KILLED THE PRINCES IN THE TOWER?

Controversy over who murdered Edward, Prince of Wales, and Richard, Duke of York, the two little sons of Edward IV, began almost immediately after their deaths in about 1485, and has continued from that day to this. There is a wealth of contemporary evidence about the mystery, some of it conflicting, and nearly all of it biased. Perhaps the most important in the sixteenth century, and virtually unchallenged for 100 years, was The History of King Richard III, *written in 1514 by Sir Thomas More. Unfortunately, at the time of the events of which he wrote, More was only five years old. In fact he based his work largely on the writings of Thomas Morton, unprincipled and careerist Bishop of Ely, later to become one of Henry VII's chief ministers.* Both these accounts were deeply hostile to Richard III. In 1593 William Shakespeare based his dramatic interpretation of Richard's life on*

---

* Morton was Henry's finance minister and instigator of the infamous 'Morton's Fork', whereby over-mighty noblemen were heavily fined on the grounds that if they lived lavishly they must be rich and so could afford to 'fork out', while if they lived frugally they must have a lot of money saved up and so could *still* afford the fine.

such histories. Shakespeare took the classical pro-
Tudor stance in damning Richard, portraying him as
the ultimate villain, sadistic and pitiless, yet at the
same time giving him a streak of malicious humour.
Such accounts as these have no room for doubt
about who killed the princes in the Tower.

But almost from the beginning there was another school
of opinion. Voices questioning Richard's guilt were
raised as early as 1500, but the first full statement of the
revisionist case was made in 1622 by the Jacobean
historian Sir George Buck in his monumental five-
volume work *The History of the Reign of Henry VII.*
Others followed in the eighteenth and nineteenth
centuries. Perhaps the most interesting of the modern
accounts is *The Daughter of Time* by Josephine Tey, who
rewrote the mystery as a detective story in 1951. Her
book was closely followed by the more scholarly
Richard the Third, written in 1955 by Paul Murray
Kendall and often regarded as the definitive biography
of the king, though revisionist in tone. These authors
rebutted the charges against Richard, denying that he
was a villain – or even a hunchback – and painting him
as a conscientious man whose reputation was irremedi-
ably blackened in a brazen libel stemming from Tudor
malevolence.

Though repeatedly resolved to the satisfaction of both
the Tudor and Yorkist sides, for others the case of the
princes in the Tower still remains a historical mystery.
The Yorkist account of the reign, and that of the later
White Rose Society, says Richard III was wickedly
maligned and was innocent of the charge of having procured the deaths of the princes. The Yorkists pointed out
that the popular version of this story was owed largely to

Shakespeare. He wrote his play in the reign of Queen Elizabeth, and his pro-Tudor views, springing partly out of a fashionable desire to flatter the queen, helped to shape later generations' monstrous image of Richard. As the need to butter up the Tudors declined after the death of Elizabeth I in 1603, so the revisionist school took new heart and set about the task of rehabilitating the unfortunate Richard. They showed that in fact he sprang from a secure and happy family background, and soon revealed himself a gifted soldier and an effective, if rather strait-laced, political administrator. He was deeply loyal to his brother Edward IV, a dazzlingly successful monarch who nevertheless allowed himself to be manipulated by women – especially the women he adored. This aspect of Edward's character revealed itself when he married Elizabeth Woodville and brought the ambitious Woodville family into prominence. When Edward unexpectedly died in 1483, his will instructed that Richard be Lord Protector until Edward, Prince of Wales, could be crowned king.

Almost immediately the machinations of the Woodville family were revealed. Richard took prompt action, arresting and later executing several of them. He took charge of the two princes and committed them to the secure royal residence of the Tower of London, where they remained under guard for the rest of their lives. At the time the protector's actions were far from unpopular. England saw what the Woodvilles were up to, and the vast majority preferred to rally to the brother of the former king rather than to those of the former queen.

Shortly afterwards, however, Richard learned from Robert Stillington, Bishop of Bath and Wells, that before the Woodville marriage Edward IV had entered into a 'pre-contract'* with Lady Eleanor Butler, a minor scion of the country aristocracy from Gloucestershire. In view of this, Richard deposed both princes, sons of Elizabeth Woodville, on grounds of their illegitimacy, and assumed the throne himself.

Richard was not vindictive towards his defeated rivals, however. In spite of her mistrust of his actions he remained on good terms with Elizabeth Woodville herself, providing her with accommodation after she quit sanctuary in Westminster Abbey. At this time she also handed over to him her four younger sisters and her daughter Elizabeth. Richard awarded the queen a yearly pension of 700 marks. He also showed forbearance towards the other members of her family.

In 1484 the only parliament of his reign passed an Act of Settlement known as the *Titulus Regius*, confirming Richard's title to the throne. The king went on to instruct Parliament to pass a whole raft of measures beneficial to the country, including reform of the land-tenure system, restriction of livery and maintenance,**

---

  * Such pre-contracts were not unusual at the time, and were generally regarded as binding. The agreement meant that, in return for a promise of later formal marriage, Edward entered into full sexual relations with his fiancée, who thus became his wife in all but name.

** Livery referred to the common practice by the aristocracy of keeping uniformed servants (sometimes under arms), who might easily form the nucleus of a private army to enforce a supremacy over local rivals; maintenance was the practice of maintaining private suitors in court and appropriating the rewards of successful suits, which enabled powerful people to interfere with the course of justice, for example, by intimidating juries and even royal judges.

and the abolition of the hated system of compulsory payment of 'benevolences' to the sovereign.* All of this earned him the title of 'especial good lord'. His government was popular and certainly stood in no danger from the two young princes in the Tower. So he had no reason to wish them dead. None of those who maligned his character seemed to question why, if the boys were no threat to him, he should want to murder them.

Richard's critics alleged that he ordered one of his followers, Tyrell, to relieve Sir Thomas Brackenbury as Governor of the Tower, and instructed his henchmen Catesby and Ratcliffe (the *cat* and the *rat* 'who governed all England under the *Hog*', i.e. the wild boar on York's coat of arms) to smother the boys with pillows and dispose of their bodies. It is significant that no such charge was made against him during his lifetime, and that even after his defeat and death at the battle of Bosworth in 1485 at the hands of his arch-rival Henry Tudor, the matter of the alleged murder was never so much as mentioned in the bill of attainder brought against him by his successor. The rumours began to spread only in the reign of Henry VII when Richard was no longer there to rebut them.

After Bosworth, Henry, with only the slightest claim to the throne of England himself (his mother was the heir of an illegitimate son of the third son of Edward III), ruled the country by conquest and in his own right, until he reinforced his claims shortly after his

---

* Benevolences were forced loans extorted from the gentry and the well-to-do, supposedly as voluntary contributions towards the upkeep of a popular but needy monarch. This was where Morton wielded his notorious 'fork'.

succession by marrying the eighteen-year-old Elizabeth of York, who was sister to the two princes in the Tower. Henry then got Parliament to repeal the *Titulus Regius* and to suppress all existing copies of the act. His aim was to strengthen the hold his military victory had brought him. He could not so strengthen his claims if the princess was illegitimate; but if on the other hand she was legitimate, so were the princes, and they had a better claim to the throne than he did. So, the Yorkists and the revisionists say, he was obliged to destroy them, and to shift the blame on to Richard. It is interesting that, far from condemning Tyrell for his treasonable actions, Henry later actually rewarded him with a provincial governorship in France and a series of senior appointments in the field of diplomacy. Later Henry went on to eliminate many remaining Yorkists whose claims to the throne were better than his own: the young Edward, Earl of Warwick, and John, Earl of Lincoln, son of John de la Pole, Duke of Suffolk, and after him his younger brother Edmund, Earl of Suffolk. All these were called upon to pay with their lives the price of the new king's tyranny. Henry was thus able to unite the Red Rose of Lancaster with the White Rose of York, and so lay the foundations of Tudor rule in England throughout the sixteenth century.

The classical account of the murders of the two young princes – the view put forward by the defenders of the Red Rose of Lancaster, and still accepted by many – places the blame squarely on the shoulders of Richard III. Edward IV's unexpected demise and the widespread unpopularity of the Woodville clique presented Richard with his opportunity to rid the country of the entire family. He hastened down from York while the Woodvilles were bringing the young Edward back from

Ludlow, meeting them at Stony Stratford and taking the boy under his protection. Richard escorted Edward to London and lodged him in the royal apartments in the Tower; then he moved swiftly against the Woodvilles. Anthony Woodville, the queen's brother, was executed without trial, and Lord Hastings, realising that Richard was aiming at the throne, was seized and executed. Thereafter Richard tried to discredit the reputation of Edward IV himself. When this ploy failed, he broadcast the belief that Edward V was illegitimate because his father had entered into a marriage pre-contract with Lady Butler. Hence Parliament was persuaded to recognise Richard's claim in the act *Titulus Regius* and deposed Edward on 25 June 1483, proclaiming his uncle king next day. By the standards of the time, such action was understandable, if not justified: dynastic rivalry was not at an end, and England needed a ruler with full authority. Richard felt he had to depose the king and eliminate the Woodvilles, whom he abominated, so as to restore the country to stability and peace.

With the young Edward V deposed, the question remains why Richard felt he and his brother should be killed. Those who argue, like the revisionists, that Richard had no reason to murder them do not take into account the grim realities of late fifteenth-century politics: he kept them in close confinement precisely because they were such a danger to him, and then did away with them secretly in case they should be the focus of a later coup against him. The murder of a ruling monarch – or a deposed one – was not in any way unusual: such a fate had already befallen Edward II, Richard II and Henry VI. Furthermore, Richard had already dealt harshly with Hastings, Rivers and others of the Woodvilles, and was commonly acknowledged as ruthless. Kings had to be ruthless in those days if they were to survive. But as a result of his brutality his popularity declined, especially in the south where his northern supporters were regarded as barbarians. In fact there had already been suggestions of restoring the youthful Edward V to the throne. Furthermore, Richard may have felt that the act of Parliament that had removed Edward's legitimacy could easily be revoked: as long as the princes were alive they were a threat to him and his control of the kingdom.

It seems likely that Richard ordered the boys' deaths in the late summer of 1483 while he was on a state tour of his realm and outside the capital. Although rumours were rife about the princes' fate, the real facts about their murders were unknown and no one dared challenge the king over their whereabouts. Indeed their fate was not discussed in public until after Richard's death, and the bodies were not discovered until their bones were dug up from under a staircase during a refurbishment of the Tower in the reign of Charles II, nearly 200 years later.

Richard's critics contend that it was the increasing unpredictability of his behaviour after 1483 that led to the steady swelling of popular discontent. This also helps to explain his apparent benevolence at the time of his parliament: he was desperately anxious that his people should overcome their mistrust of him and accept his rule. One of the main threats at the time came from his former supporter Henry Stafford, Duke of Buckingham, who before 1485 had taken the precaution of entering into an alliance with the upstart Woodvilles and with the ambitious Henry Tudor, currently biding his time in France awaiting his opportunity to return. Henry was said already to be planning to marry the young Elizabeth of York, though significantly not until after he had won the throne because he did not wish to be ruling the country solely by the right of his wife. This explains why Richard, who had recently lost his own wife Anne Neville (and also incidentally about the same time his heir to the throne, the young Richard, Prince of Wales), was so especially nice to Elizabeth Woodville when she came out of sanctuary – he seems to have been contemplating an incestuous marriage with his own niece. Declaring the princes illegitimate and killing them, and then marrying their sister seemed monstrous even to Richard's most loyal supporters, and Elizabeth Woodville, ambitious for a return to power as she was, found his actions quite unendurable.

Henry's plans for a rebellion came to fruition in August 1485 when he invaded England with a miscellaneous band of followers and met Richard at Market Bosworth, just west of Leicester. Richard was a brave soldier and a skilled commander, and would almost certainly have won the ensuing battle had it not been for the treachery of Lord Stanley, Earl of Derby – one of those whom the king had recently pardoned as a member of the Woodville faction. At the last moment Derby defected to the Tudor side and precipitated Richard's defeat. The king rode straight into the thick of the fight, but without Derby's support he was unhorsed, surrounded and finally killed. His naked body was carried on a packhorse to Leicester for burial; his crown, according to tradition, was found under a thorn bush and placed on Henry's head. With his death the line of York came to an end. Henry declared Richard's actions treasonable, and, because it was a logical impossibility for Richard to commit treason against himself, dated his own reign from the day before the battle of Bosworth.

Common rumour that the princes were dead now began to surface, but Henry was unsure of the boys' fates and hence he did not accuse Richard of having killed them when the act of attainder against him was passed into law. Henry did reduce Elizabeth Woodville's pension to 400 marks a year and confiscated all her estates. But he did not take any action against Tyrell, who continued as Governor of Guisnes in the Pale of Calais (a post he had taken under Richard III). Tyrell was condemned and executed only in 1502 after he became involved in an overseas rising by Edmund, Earl of Suffolk (younger brother of John, Earl of Lincoln, who had perished in the rebellion against Henry at the battle of Stoke in 1487). In the same spirit of letting sleeping dogs lie and in the interests of maintaining his wife Elizabeth's dignity, Henry likewise made no mention of Richard's earlier intention of marrying her. His main aim was to re-establish peace and security in England as quickly as possible, and so he avoided stirring up the mud for fear of what might be revealed.

After examining the arguments for both sides, the conclusion has to be that the mystery surrounding the deaths of the princes in the Tower remains unsolved. Their story still occasions debate between committed Lancastrians and Yorkists, generating perhaps more heat than light. The end of the Wars of the Roses marked the crucial turning-point of modern British history; but no definitive proof of the identity of the party guilty of the twin murders of the princes Edward and Richard has ever come to light, nor is it likely now that it will.

HAS THE DEATH OF GEORGE II BEEN FICTIONALISED?

The manner of George II's death has provided historians with an opportunity to indulge their fancies, sometimes improperly. Efforts have been made to engage in malicious tittle-tattle at the poor man's expense, or even to make a joke of his demise. In fact, in spite of all the unfounded rumours, the circumstances of his death were much less mysterious than has often been supposed.

George II was not the most attractive of monarchs. He was rude and choleric. He never forgot an injury or forgave an insult, and he was not gifted with high intelligence. He could be obstinate: he refused clemency to Admiral Byng who was shot in 1757 for negligence in battle, but was really executed as a scapegoat for an incompetent government; the king resisted the intense political pressure to reprieve him. George also refused office to the elder Pitt when there seemed no other worthy choice. Apart from his patronage of Handel, he had little interest in the arts or literature, nor did he show filial or parental affection. His quarrel with his son Frederick reached scandalous dimensions. In his treatment of his wife he showed lack of tact. Even though she was dying of cancer, it was a long time before George accepted that his wife Caroline was really ill. As she lay dying she urged the now remorseful George to take another wife. 'No, I shall have mistresses,' was his reply. What consolation was that for the stricken woman?

Unable to find any light relief in the dour George's life, contemporaries and historians have made a comedy out of his death. The king died on the morning of 25 October 1760. His servants were at first sworn to secrecy as to the manner of his demise, but within a few hours the details emerged. George had enjoyed his usual morning chocolate at 7 a.m. He had then gone into his closet to relieve himself. Hardly had the valet closed the door when he heard a noise and a thud. He hastily pushed the door open to find that George had collapsed, and in falling had hit his head on the cupboard just inside the closet. He had not had time to reach the inner sanctum which contained the toilet seat. Attempts were made to revive the king with the usual bloodlettings and application of leeches, but all to no avail. George had died of a stroke.

Some malicious gossips soon put it about that George had died from his exertions and straining on the toilet. (It was well known that he suffered from constipation, common among the upper classes whose rich, protein-heavy diet lacked balance – they consumed very little fruit.) This imaginative version of events was not backed by any of the king's servants, but originated from second-hand gossip. Yet it has been adopted by some historians, including Professor J.H. Plumb in *The First Four Georges*. Unless they were lying, the evidence of George's servants is fairly unanimous and supports the version of events which has it that the king's fatal seizure occurred as soon as he entered the closet. Royal servants were not noted in the eighteenth century for their loyalty, and had George's death been more colourful it is hardly credible that its circumstances would not soon have become public knowledge. There is no specific testimony to this effect; the more dramatic account can only be considered corroborative detail for which there is no supporting evidence.

DID THE DAUPHIN PERISH IN THE FRENCH REVOLUTION?

In the years after the Terror a mystery grew up concerning the fate of the dauphin, who should have become King Louis XVII of France on the execution of his father in 1793. It was said that the young dauphin had somehow managed to survive the dank filth of his cell in the Temple (the prison were he was housed) and the crude ministrations of the Paris cobbler and his wife who were his jailers, and had made his escape to freedom. From time to time the story was elaborated with the suggestion that Robespierre himself had taken pity on the boy and had connived at his flight.

According to those who accepted this version of events, the boy was said to have been brought up in obscurity in the French countryside and only later to have found out that he was the rightful king. After 1815 a number of royal claimants, including a stable boy and a Prussian clockmaker, came forward as pretenders. This clockmaker was so convincing that he persuaded the now rather elderly Versailles maid who had attended the young prince to say that she recognised him. As a result, he secured cautious acceptance by King Louis Philippe and was awarded a small pension by him. He went on to live in obscurity in the Netherlands, and when he died in 1840 he was buried at Delft under the epitaph 'Here Lies Louis XVII, Duke of Normandy, King of France and of Navarre'. The idea of the dauphin's dramatic escape from his jailers was later taken up by Baroness d'Orczy, who described the episode in her *Scarlet Pimpernel* stories, where she alleged that the boy had been helped to escape and had been whisked away to his relatives in Austria.

The truth is equally exciting, and scarcely less incredible. The royal prince, always a delicate child, had succumbed to tuberculosis in the damp conditions of his cell at the age of ten in 1795, and was buried under the name of Louis Charles Capet in a mass grave in that year. Before the interment there had been an inquest. The doctor involved, a man by the name of Pelletan, a royalist, had filched the child's heart at the autopsy, concealed it in his handkerchief and later passed it to the Archbishop of Paris, who kept it in a jar until his cathedral was attacked and looted during the 1830 revolution. The jar was smashed, but Pelletan's son picked up the mummified remains of the heart and kept it in a crystal urn. It was subjected to DNA tests in 1999 and samples compared with Louis's mother's hair, that of two of her sisters, and the hair of two of the family's living relatives.

The tests proved beyond all reasonable doubt that the dauphin had died in 1795, and the heart was his. In the nineteenth century the grave in which his remains had been placed was excavated twice, and on both occasions the bones were said to have belonged to a much older boy of about seventeen. The results of the DNA tests, however, are now accepted as definitive.

WAS NAPOLEON MURDERED?

St Helena is a rainy, windswept island deep in the South Atlantic, used by the British in the nine-teenth century as a staging post for ships bound for

India and Australia. It was here that Napoleon I of France spent nearly six years in exile, and here that he died on 5 May 1821. But what was the cause of his death?

It was not long before rumours began alleging that Napoleon had not died of natural causes. After all, he was only in his early fifties, and both his French entourage and his British guardians had much to gain by his death: they could go home. Poison, either arsenic or strychnine, administered over time was alleged to have killed him.

The French accused the British of deliberately revenging themselves on Napoleon for the long period of warfare to which he had subjected Britain and the rest of Europe. This seems highly unlikely. The Tory government of Lord Liverpool may have been reactionary but it was not given to political assassination. The need for such extreme action was negligible: it was extremely improbable that a bunch of French desperadoes would try to rescue Napoleon from such a remote island, right under the noses of the British navy. Nor was the French Bourbon government anxious to see Napoleon's fortunes restored. And Britain's agent for murder, should the government have felt so inclined, would have been a particularly unsuitable choice. Sir Hudson Lowe, the Governor of St Helena, kept strictly and unimaginatively to the letter of his instructions, and lacked both the initiative to commit murder on his own account and the villainy to do so secretly on behalf of the government. His subordinates, both civilian and military, were on limited postings and expected to go home when their time was completed. They had no particular incentive to see Napoleon dead.

Not so the Frenchmen who shared Napoleon's exile. They would be obliged out of loyalty to stay on St Helena and serve him until the end. But all Napoleon's entourage were so devoted to him that it is impossible to find a murder suspect among them. Accusations against General Montholon, who was one of the former emperor's companions and quarrelled with him, lack supporting evidence. Disagreements among the exiles were only to be expected under the circumstances and are not in themselves indicative of a greater likelihood of murder. It has recently been suggested that Montholon or one of his aides was in a secret plot with Charles, the Bourbon heir to the French throne, to murder Napoleon. The evidence is thin and circumstantial: Montholon may well have wanted to return to France, but it seems highly improbable that he would have countenanced treachery and murder to do so.

However, there is no doubt that quite early on in his exile Napoleon became convinced that the British were trying to kill him. He complained that Hudson Lowe placed restrictions on his exercise, although the gout was more effective in doing that. He complained of the cold and the damp, said that sunlight gave him headaches, and suffered from sore and bleeding gums. His doctor, Barry O'Meara, was less convinced of the patient's good health than was Hudson Lowe, and when Lowe discovered that O'Meara was sending private reports of Napoleon's health back to Europe, he had him dismissed in July 1818. A naval doctor named Stokoe reported that Napoleon was suffering from hepatitis. Then a doctor from Corsica, Francesco Antommarchi, arrived in 1819, and for a time accounts of Napoleon's health were more encouraging.

But by 1820 Dr Antommarchi was reporting that his patient was shivering and suffered feverishness, biliousness, coughing, nausea and vomiting. These symptoms came more frequently and with greater severity during Napoleon's last months. In his final hours Napoleon was rambling and incoherent, but his symptoms gave no clear indication as to the nature and cause of his malady.

The post-mortem was conducted by both British and French doctors, who naturally disagreed on the cause of death. The French doctors claimed that Napoleon's health had been undermined by so long a sojourn in such an unhealthy place. They pointed out his ulcerated stomach – Antommarchi pushed his finger through the perforated stomach in dramatic support of his diagnosis. But the English doctors insisted that he had been suffering from stomach cancer, for which the climate of St Helena and the conditions of his captivity could not be held responsible.

The discovery, with the aid of modern analysis methods, of traces of arsenic in Napoleon's hair has not advanced the argument much. Small amounts of the poison were a common ingredient of some of the medicines of the time, and certainly the paste holding up the wallpaper in Napoleon's room contained it. Arsenic contamination can occur both before and after death, and it is not possible to point the finger with any certainty at who administered it, if indeed it was administered and not acquired naturally. It seems far more likely that Napoleon was not poisoned, but died of some kind of stomach complaint, whether cancer or severe ulceration. Those who assert otherwise still have to prove their case.

HOW DID RASPUTIN DIE?

Mystery surrounds the murder in 1916 of Grigori Rasputin. The self-styled monk was a scruffy and revolting libertine given to orgies of sex and drink. Yet he was also a friend of the tsarina and chief adviser to Tsar Nicholas II on the eve of the Russian revolutions of 1917. What is the truth behind all the conflicting stories?

In the 1920s an action was brought in London before Mr Justice Avory by Prince Yusupov, with Sir Patrick Hastings appearing for the plaintiff, against the Metro-Goldwyn-Mayer Corporation of America in respect of a film made by that company about Rasputin. In this film he was portrayed as the lover of Princess Yusupov, a claim which she and her husband strenuously denied. The story is told in Sir Patrick's memoirs, published in 1949 under the title *Cases in Court*. Both the princess and the prince were impressive in the witness box, and they won damages from the film company of the (then) enormous sum of £25,000. Free from any threat of prosecution in Britain after the Russian Bolshevik revolution, Yusupov was asked a direct question by his counsel as he gave his evidence; he said, quite frankly, 'Yes, I killed Rasputin. It was my duty to kill him. So I killed him.'

He told how a group of Russian nobles decided in December 1916 to assassinate him. They were disturbed at Rasputin's hold over the tsarina – who seems to have become convinced that he alone could alleviate her son's haemophilia – and anxious lest his wild and irresponsible decisions would take Russia out of the First World War or set the upper classes on a path to destruction. The task of assassination would not be easy. Superstition claimed that the intended victim had trained himself to be impervious to poison, and that not even bullets could harm him. In fact it was believed Rasputin could not die. All the same, he was invited to the Yusupov's own Moika Palace on the pretence of enjoying one of those drunken orgies in which he revelled, and there he was done to death.

When the victim arrived, gramophone music was playing, supposedly for his entertainment but really to prevent the outside world from hearing any noise during the struggle that followed. He was taken by his host to one of the palace's lower rooms, where he was met by prostitutes and regaled with the sweet cakes he so enjoyed. The cakes were soaked in enough cyanide to kill a dozen men, but Rasputin wolfed them one by one, apparently without ill effect. Yusupov was unnerved; he rushed for a revolver and shot his victim from behind. When Rasputin fell, Yusupov felt sure that he was dead, but he returned with a fellow-conspirator, Vladimir Purishkevich, to confirm the deed. The wounded man suddenly reared up and staggered from the room into the courtyard where Purishkevich, too, shot him with his own revolver. During the 1920s libel trial it was claimed that the conspirators had also beaten Rasputin with a loaded stick. Then they dumped the body into the ice-bound River Neva. But when it was recovered, there was water in the lungs. When he hit the water, Rasputin had not been dead, Yusupov said; he had drowned by immersion in the freezing river. Possibly because of the universal hatred in which Rasputin was held, the only action the tsar took against Yusupov was to exile him to a remote part of his estate in rural Russia.

Yusupov's testimony in the MGM libel trial created a sensation in Britain. He was only able to give it because he knew that the Bolsheviks would never prosecute him for such a patriotic act – in any case, they could not get their hands on him in Britain, and Britain was unlikely to surrender him even if asked to do so. The story was so bizarre that it needed no embellishment. It was widely reported in the press, and the records of the case are still in existence.

But was any of Yusupov's account true? Police archives, re-examined by an eminent Russian pathologist, Professor Vladimir Zharov, in 1994, and again in 2004 by a senior British police officer, Richard Cullen, formerly Commander of the Metropolitan Police, tell a different story of the murder. Rasputin had been lured to the palace so as to separate him from his usual bodyguard, and there he was received in a basement room. There was music, but no prostitutes. Masked men emerged from the palace after two hours, not the four hours Yusupov claimed had been necessary to subdue the victim. They were carrying a body, which they dumped in the river. Post-mortem findings and photographs, still on record, show that the man died of gunshot wounds, two from behind, the first bullet passing through the stomach and finishing up in the liver, and the other coming to rest in the kidneys. These alone were enough to kill him after a few minutes, but there was a third wound made by a larger calibre bullet and unexplained in Yusupov's account. It was in the centre of the forehead and had critically damaged the brain. This wound seemed to have been administered by a professional assassin. Forensic examination found no traces of poison in the body, nor, apart from minor abrasions, any trace of the physical beating Rasputin was said to have received.

Cullen's inquiry pointed strongly to the involvement of espionage agents in the killing. In 1916 British intelligence agents, acting quite independently of the British government (though with its tacit approval), were intriguing strongly against Rasputin's influence over the tsar's government, since it was widely suspected he was trying to pull Russia out of the First World War and this would have exposed the Allied powers to increased German pressure on the Western Front. The British SIS (Secret Intelligence Service, the forerunner of MI6) had allotted at least two officers to the task of monitoring Rasputin's influence over the Russian royal family. Based at the SIS HQ in the Astoria Hotel in St Petersburg, the two most significant British intelligence operatives were John Scale, at the time attached to the tsar's staff at the front and several hundred miles away, and his junior officer, Oswald Rayner, who had infiltrated the conspirators' circle and who was not only privy to their plans to remove the man they codenamed 'Dark Forces', but was actually present at the time of, or shortly after, the murder. Surviving intelligence records seem to point pretty definitely to the conclusion that it was Rayner whose bullet inflicted the final *coup de grâce* on Rasputin in the courtyard.

Yusupov, who died in 1967, never retracted his story of the murder, though the account he gave of it differs substantially from the one in Purishkevich's memoirs and from the police records in the St Petersburg Museum of History. Furthermore, from time to time Yusupov changed the details of his account (though he does mention Oswald Rayner in his own memoirs). His version of events was never challenged until recently, but it is now generally agreed that the real story was much more strange: Rasputin's supposed powers were mythical – in fact, according to *Times* reporter Byran Moynahan, 'the records show that the legend of invincibility was false, and was perpetuated by those who killed him' – but British military intelligence was closely connected with the murder.

WHAT WAS THE FATE OF ADOLF HITLER?

Everyone who has studied GCSE history knows very well what happened to Adolf Hitler, Führer of the Third Reich, in 1945. There seems to be no possible mystery about his gruesome end. And yet, have they been told the whole story about what many school textbooks dismiss in a single sentence?

By April 1945 the Russian armies of Marshal Zhukov and Marshal Koniev, nearly half a million men in number, were at the outskirts of Berlin, and Hitler, in spite of insistent advice from his advisers to quit the city and to take command of the counter-attack to save the capital, was cut off and surrounded in the area of the Reichs Chancellery. He, together with Eva Braun and his advisers, took refuge in a two-storey defensive bunker 60 feet down, likened by one of them to a concrete submarine on account of its inefficient air-conditioning.

The 20th was his fifty-sixth birthday. The very next day the Soviet armies launched their final attack on Berlin, but the SS counter-attack by General Steiner did not materialise. Hitler was beside himself with rage. He fumed and ranted at all around him, vowing to stay in Berlin until it fell and then to shoot himself. Senior army officers Wilhelm Keitel and Alfred Jodl were disgusted at his unprofessional behaviour: it was his duty to give orders and take responsibility, they felt, not to behave like a hysterical prima donna.

Goering suggested on the 22nd that he be given a chance to offer peace to the Western allies, but Hitler responded by dismissing him from all his appointments and ordering his immediate arrest for treason. On the 23rd even Himmler contemplated making peace behind Hitler's back and had secret meetings with Count Bernadotte at the Swedish Embassy. Himmler's representative with the Führer, Hermann Fegelein, who had slipped out of the bunker with a view to making his escape, was arrested, his pockets full of jewellery, and was hauled back to the Chancellery courtyard and shot, in spite of the fact that his mistress was Eva Braun's sister Gretl.

Hitler, on the uncertain line between sanity and insanity, dithered and ranted for days. He made grandiose plans, drank champagne and did nothing. On the 29th he wrote his political testament, making arrangements for the government after his death and swearing his undying hatred for 'international Jewry'; then he willed his few possessions to those close to him. He learned, with little apparent emotion, of the death of Mussolini and his mistress Clara Petacci, and swore for his own part that he would never become 'an animal on show at the Moscow Zoo'. In the early hours of the 30th he married Eva Braun. She swore to remain with him in the Führerbunker and to share his fate, whatever that was.

On the 30th he said goodbye to his staff, had a quiet lunch with Frau Hitler, and ordered his valet and his chauffeur to bring 200 litres of petrol to the garden above the bunker. His valet carried out his orders, though it was difficult to find such a large quantity of petrol at such short notice. The couple retired to the Führer's suite and his valet heard a single shot. When he opened the door he found Hitler lying with a gunshot wound to his head. Eva had taken poison. With some difficulty the bodies were carried upstairs and placed in a hole at the bottom of a Russian shell crater. They were doused in petrol and incinerated as artillery shells fell nearby. That evening Soviet soldiers planted the red flag on top of the Reichstag building.

However, the story of Hitler's demise was marked by inconsistencies and uncertainties from the very beginning. Was Hitler really dead or did he effect a miraculous escape? Did he shoot himself through the mouth, as was originally maintained, or through the temple, or the forehead? Were the two bodies completely consumed by the burning petrol, or was this impossible in such conditions in the open air? Were the bodies covered with earth as they lay, or were they properly buried in the Chancellery grounds? Did Hitler's body really fall into Russian hands, or was it too difficult to pick out the right corpse from the many others at the same spot? Did the Russians perhaps allow themselves to be fobbed off with a Hitler double?

All these questions have been asked, and, more than half a century after the event, are now impossible to answer with any certainty. Witnesses, including Hitler's valet, Heinz Linge, who was still alive in 2003, testified that Hitler took poison as well as shooting himself. Linge said that he himself burned the two bodies as best he could with something short of 200 litres of petrol and then helped to bury them in the Chancellery garden, where the Russians never found them. The Russians did not enter the Führerbunker until 2 May, when women orderlies of the Soviet Medical Corps explored it and carried off Eva Hitler's lacy underwear as trophies of war. Bunker staff were rounded up for questioning by the secret police acting on Stalin's urgent instructions – he wanted to get hold of Hitler's body. Rooting about, they found numerous bodies, including those of Goebbels (Hitler's propaganda chief) and his wife and six children. They also found a Hitler double, bobbing about in a water tank near the bunker with a bullet hole in his forehead (Stalin refused to believe that this man was Hitler, chiefly on the strength of the fact that he wore darned socks).

For many years, the Russians denied having located the bodies at all. Stalin feared that Hitler might somehow reappear. Even if the Führer was dead, the Russian leader was anxious to avoid the creation of some kind of Napoleonic legend by neo-Nazis. Then, in 1968, a Soviet journalist, Lev Bezymenski, published a book revealing that the Russians had found the charred bodies on 4 May 1945 and taken them to a hospital under Soviet control. Dental records confirmed that the male body was Hitler's. The two were reburied in the grounds of the KGB headquarters in Magdeburg in what was to become the Russian Zone. Churchill visited them at this spot in 1945. These few remains were removed in 1970 and finally fully cremated; nothing survives. At the time of the cremation, DNA testing had not been developed. So in the absence of physical evidence, doubt must remain over whether these were in fact fragments of Hitler's body.

The written records still exist in plenty in Moscow as testament to Stalin's obsession with the death of his arch-enemy and rival. Among the records there is even a fragment of a human skull with a bullet hole in it. These, and the verbal testimony of witnesses, are all that we have to indicate the nature of Hitler's fate.

2

Mysterious Identities

WHO MURDERED LORD DARNLEY?

*In 1567 Kirk o' Field was a comfortable house of
good Scottish proportions on the outskirts of
Edinburgh. Here, a recovering invalid, Lord
Darnley, was housed to avoid the stagnant and
damp city air of Holyrood Palace. At about 2 a.m.
on the morning of 10 February a huge explosion
reduced Kirk o' Field to rubble, killing several
domestics, but not Darnley and his valet; they were
found 60 yards away under some bushes. They had
no marks of the explosion upon them, but they had
been strangled. It was obvious that this was a
planned and premeditated murder, but who was
responsible? Darnley was husband to Mary Queen
of Scots and to this day argument has raged over
the extent of her involvement in his murder.*

The princess Mary was born on 8 December in 1542.
Within six days her father James V was dead and she
had become queen. It was an unhappy Scotland into
which she was born. The country had just suffered a
humiliating defeat at the hands of the English at
Solway Moss. Many of the nobility were prisoners in
English hands. Those who had escaped capture
engaged in petty rivalries which could and often did
lead to bloodshed and open conflict. The Scottish
Church was still officially Catholic, but reformers such

as John Knox were becoming increasingly powerful and were threatening to break with Rome, as England had so recently done. For the next few years young Mary was a political pawn: on the one hand the Protestant party favoured her betrothal to Prince Edward of England; on the other the Catholic party favoured a Spanish or a traditional French alliance.

When Scotland's Catholic primate, Cardinal Beaton, made himself insufferable by his burning of Protestant preachers, he was murdered in 1546. The potential for the triumph of the English party, supported by English incursions, alarmed Mary's French mother, Mary of Guise, who was acting as regent. And when the English mounted an invasion in 1547 to fetch the five-year-old Queen Mary to England, the Scots were overwhelmed at the battle of Pinkie Cleugh. The English trampled over southern Scotland, but the young queen was well protected, being concealed in west Scotland for a few crucial days.

By the beginning of 1548 Mary of Guise felt the only hope for the security of her daughter was to hurry the French alliance. French troops arrived in Scotland in considerable numbers, thus associating the Catholic religion with foreign domination and turning Protestantism into a national cause. Amid all this turmoil, young Queen Mary was sent to France in August 1548, there to be brought up as a devout Catholic and as the intended bride of Prince Francis.

Her happiest years followed, but they were not to last. In 1559 her father-in-law, Henry II, was killed in a joust by the Duc de Montgomery's lance, and her husband was now King Francis II of France. But he was weak and sickly, and in December 1560 he succumbed to an ear infection. Mary now had no valid excuse for staying in France, and her presence in her Scottish kingdom was urgently needed. Her mother's death earlier in the year had left a political vacuum there, and Scotland was now in effect governed by John Knox and his allies among the Protestant nobility. The Scottish Parliament had officially renounced Catholicism and embraced Protestantism in 1559, although the royal consent to this was lacking, and when Mary arrived in Scotland in August 1561 her first attempt to hold Mass in her private chapel was almost wrecked by rowdy reformers.

Both England and Scotland now had unmarried queens without heirs: Mary was keen to marry again, hoping that a new union would either give her a Catholic husband and a foreign alliance to tackle Protestantism in Scotland, or, if it were approved by Elizabeth, remove any threat from England and secure a possible public recognition that Mary was next in succession to the English throne. Elizabeth was, as usual, ambivalent. If Mary was to marry then Elizabeth must approve of the groom, but it might be better to procrastinate until Elizabeth herself had married and settled the succession once and for all. When Elizabeth heard that negotiations were afoot for Mary to marry Philip of Spain's heir, Don Carlos, she was alarmed. She countered by encouraging the suit of Robert Dudley, Earl of Leicester. When news of Don Carlos's mental state caused the Spanish match to cool, Elizabeth grew less keen on the Leicester alternative. She decided to muddy the waters by sending young Lord Darnley to Scotland.

Lord Darnley had both English and Scottish blood in his veins. He was descended from Henry VII of England through the second marriage of Henry's daughter Margaret, and he was related to the Stuarts. He was nearly four years younger than Mary; he was tall (like Mary), fair, handsome, and above all a Catholic. He journeyed to Scotland in February 1565. Within a few weeks Mary was infatuated with him. When news reached Elizabeth that the couple were planning to marry she realised that her schemes had misfired; instead of diverting Mary, Darnley had captivated her. Elizabeth could not prevent the marriage and it took place on 29 July 1565. The next day Mary gave Darnley the title of king, and all royal documents were henceforth in the names of Queen Mary and King Henry. In revenge Elizabeth threw Darnley's mother, the Countess of Lennox, into the Tower of London where she was to remain for six months.

Passion not politics had dictated the marriage, but passion does not always last. In this case it did not survive the autumn of 1565. Darnley was not satisfied with the mere title of king: he expected his wife to be meek and submissive and to defer to him in all matters of state. He demanded the crown matrimonial, which would make him king in fact as well as in name. But he was not really interested in affairs of state, only in the reflected glory that being king would give him. He was, by all accounts, indolent, pleasure-loving, bibulous, vain and jealous. Nor was his Catholicism reliable; he refused to join Queen Mary in the nuptial Mass after the marriage ceremony, and, perhaps to court Protestant support, he even submitted himself to one of John Knox's interminable sermons. The queen, passion cooling, began to despair of him and for support and advice turned more and more to her Italian secretary, David Rizzio (or Riccio). Once Mary found herself pregnant, Darnley's usefulness had been fulfilled and she began to exclude him from both her private and her public life.

Darnley was not the only one to become jealous of Rizzio's influence over the queen. His drinking friends saw the Italian as dangerous. So did the Protestant nobles who feared Rizzio's Catholicism. And those who were hoping to rise in the queen's favour saw Rizzio as the barrier to their advancement. When the secretary was dragged screaming from Mary's presence and murdered in an ante-room, so public a murder and so obvious an insult to the queen were undoubtedly the work of Darnley and his friends. He seems not to have thought about what the shock of it could do to a woman six months pregnant, although there is the even more sinister possibility that he had considered the consequences. After all, why murder Rizzio so publicly and in the queen's presence when he could have been so easily despatched in one of Edinburgh's dark alleys? Moreover, one of the murderers had pointed a pistol at Mary, muttering threats. Darnley, so obviously the central conspirator, entered the room immediately after the murderers had done their work, made sure that Rizzio, with nearly sixty stab wounds, was dead, and tried to ingratiate himself with Mary by naming and denouncing them. Mary had to rely on Darnley to help her escape from Holyrood to Dunbar – a five-hour ride – before the queen's supporters were sufficiently strong to enable her to re-enter Edinburgh in triumph.

After Rizzio was pronounced dead, Mary had said, 'I will then dry my tears and think of revenge.' Subsequent reconciliation with Darnley might have been expedient but could hardly have been sincere.

Mary remembered how close she had come to death when Rizzio died and at whose hands, and she was never to lose sight of revenge. Would her revenge extend to murder?

The birth of Mary's son James on 19 June 1566 made public reconciliation with Darnley very necessary. She pardoned Rizzio's murderers and let it be thought that she accepted Darnley's protestations of innocence. But when, in August 1566, Darnley complained bitterly about Mary's treatment of him, the queen's reply was revealing. He, Darnley, had abused her favours by patronising a conspiracy against her, but, notwithstanding this, she had continued to show him such respect that, though those who entered her chamber with him and murdered her faithful servant had named him as their chief, yet she had never accused him thereof, but excused him, as if she had not believed the fact. So both she and Darnley had been dissembling, he with his lies, she with her apparent acceptance of them. When Mary was taken ill at Jedburgh in October, it was ten days before Darnley was even informed.

Mary was now unwilling to place her trust in any of the Scottish lords, except her half-brother the Earl of Moray, whose life had also been in danger when Rizzio was murdered. Darnley was now threatening to kill him. As for the known murderers, most of whom had fled to England at first, they included the Lords Morton, Ruthven and Maitland. They were so angry with Darnley for betraying and abandoning them that they became obsessed with ideas for revenge. At a crucial meeting at Craigmillar in December 1566 Mary's advisers were virtually unanimous that Darnley must be removed. It was at this meeting that Bothwell first came to the fore as a man with no chequered background, and one in whom the queen could place her absolute trust. Divorce was discussed, but Mary was not keen: should it be Protestant divorce or a Catholic annulment or both, and how would it affect the legitimacy of James? When others mentioned the possibility of other methods (without specifying what they might be), Mary rebuked them, but she may not have been alert to the full implications of what they were hinting. It is virtually certain that at this meeting a bond was drawn up for the elimination of Darnley, with the loyal Bothwell as one of its leading signatories. It seemed better to them for the queen not to know of the bond or any of its details; after all, her willingness to consider divorce showed her in sympathy with the general aim of the removal of Darnley.

In January 1567 Darnley became ill of the pox (venereal rather than smallpox), and he preferred to suffer in Glasgow in the heart of Lennox country where he thought he would be safe. Rumours were already circulating that he was plotting to seize James and depose Mary, and was hoping that in this he would have the support of the Catholic powers, who were disappointed in Mary's toleration of Protestantism. He would then be king in his own right, with James as his successor. It is puzzling, therefore, to understand how Darnley was persuaded by Mary to return to Edinburgh for his convalescence, but it seems he was cajoled by her sweet words and a virtual promise of the restoration of conjugal relations. With the queen in his arms Darnley expected to be king in fact as well as in name, and the risky attempt to seize James and depose Mary would become unnecessary. Holyrood was considered too unhealthy for a recuperating invalid, so locations on the outskirts of Edinburgh were suggested.

Kirk o' Field was Darnley's choice, unwilling as he was to be housed by any of his enemies.

Since he would be returning to Holyrood very shortly, where the queen's guards and public comings and goings might make assassination difficult, the subscribers to the bond had to act quickly before Darnley left Kirk o' Field. The mistake in dealing with Rizzio had been that the murder was very public, and, with so many witnesses, the murderers were easy to identify. This time, whatever the suspicions, Darnley was to be eliminated in such a way that there were no witnesses and no proof. So gunpowder was decided upon. Huge quantities were procured and stored in the house next to Kirk o' Field. The gunpowder was transferred into the vaults of Kirk o' Field, probably on Sunday 9 February – any earlier would have increased the risk of discovery. So when the queen arrived in the early evening to spend time with Darnley, even intending to stay overnight, she was probably unaware of the impending catastrophe in the vaults two floors below. Or if she was aware of it, she showed a remarkable degree of calmness. And she would have stayed the night had she not been reminded that she was due to put in an appearance at the wedding masque of one of her favourite servants. She left for Holyrood at some time before eleven o'clock. Had she stayed the gunpowder would have been wasted, since Darnley was due to leave the next day.

After Mary left, the conspirators were quick to move into action; too quick perhaps. It seems that Darnley saw something that alarmed him, most likely some of his enemies lurking around the house. He must have moved fast, expecting treachery and aiming to get away as soon as possible. He probably had no inkling of the gunpowder. But he and his valet, still carrying Darnley's cloak, were soon spotted, overpowered and despatched by strangulation. This must have happened very close to the time planned for the explosion, because Bothwell could not have been informed of what had transpired in the garden before he set off the fuse. Had there been more time the bodies would surely have been taken back into the house so that the explosion could help to conceal the cause of death.

Confusion followed the explosion. It was some hours before it became clear that Darnley had been strangled. Mary seemed convinced that the explosion had been aimed at her, and it was nearly a week before popular opinion and public placards laid the murder at Bothwell's door. At this juncture Mary needed to keep a cool head. Whether or not she was implicated in Darnley's death, it was important that she should at least appear innocent. Moray had been out of Edinburgh at the time of the murder, fortuitously visiting his 'sick' wife. He may not have been fully involved, but he must have known that something was planned. Almost all the other ministers were deeply involved. They now offered a £2,000 reward for bringing to justice perpetrators of the crime for which they themselves were responsible. Then on 16 February they openly accused Bothwell and three of his servants of the murder.

Bothwell offered himself up for trial in April, but since Lennox (Darnley's father) and other hostile witnesses were unwilling to journey from the safety of their lands to Edinburgh the case collapsed through lack of evidence. Shortly afterwards Bothwell kidnapped Mary, carried her off to Dunbar castle, kept her there for five days, and probably ravished her. Even so, no supporters came to her assistance; public opinion

had already condemned her. Bothwell's existing
marriage was dissolved on 8 May and a week later he
married Mary. Her defenders say she had no option but
to acquiesce and she was under pressure from
ministers who were urging her to the marriage. But
within three weeks the ministers had called Scotland
to arms, ostensibly to liberate the queen from the evil
Bothwell, but in practice to depose her and set up a
Protestant regency for her son James. From this
followed military defeat, imprisonment in Loch Leven
Castle and escape to England to seek Elizabeth's help.
And from here on we are faced with contaminated
evidence, lack of information, and false witness, so that
it is virtually impossible to disentangle the truth.

Elizabeth was in a dilemma. She shrank from handing
Mary over to her Scottish enemies and probable death;
she would not restore Mary with English troops because
this would make her a dangerous rival and might lead
to the restoration of Catholicism in Scotland; and to
allow her to go to France to seek aid would be to revive
the old French–Scottish alliance which had caused
England so much grief in the past. So, as usual, she
decided to play for time. A court of inquiry was set up
in York to determine the extent, if any, of Mary's
involvement in the murder of her husband. The
Scottish witnesses lied through their teeth; the Scottish
lords were trying to shift culpability from themselves to
Bothwell and Mary, and they took care to execute
Bothwell's servants. Their evidence, despite being
extracted under torture, might have been too
incriminating to be made public, so it was never
produced.

The famous casket letters were offered to the court.
These were intended to establish Mary's guilt beyond

doubt; the ones that did were obvious forgeries, and the ones that did not were probably genuine, although they had been tampered with. Only copies have survived, so none have been subjected to modern forensic scrutiny. The members of the Scottish nobility who then or later, like Bothwell, produced their own version of events were all attempting self-justification.

So the truth will never be known. To the end of her life Mary strenuously denied involvement in Darnley's murder. This was probably a half-truth. She certainly wanted to be rid of the troublesome man. She would have preferred to end her marriage without bloodshed, but the murder of Rizzio and the threat to James rankled with her, and she was aware that at least some of the nobles had other methods in mind. She can be absolved from direct responsibility for the deployment of gunpowder and from collusion with Bothwell, but not from much else.

WHO WAS THE MAN IN THE IRON MASK?

Alexandre Dumas was a historical novelist with a vivid imagination, and it is only too easy to dismiss his Man in the Iron Mask as a figment of it. Not so; his novel was based on historical fact, but who the mysterious masked prisoner was has been an unsolved mystery for more than three centuries.

Not only did seventeenth-century travellers to France return home with stories about a political prisoner of Louis XIV whose face was always hidden and who was permanently guarded by two men ready to kill him should he unmask, but there was also a 1698 diary entry made by the lieutenant of the Bastille concerning this prisoner. He reported that the new governor of the Bastille, Saint-Mars, had brought such a prisoner with him from his previous command on the island of Sainte Marguerite in the Bay of Cannes, where he had served since 1681. The ageing prisoner remained in the Bastille for five years, and was reported to have died in November 1703. The parish register recorded his name as Marchioly. All traces of the prisoner were removed immediately after his death; his few belongings were destroyed, and his room was redecorated and refurbished. References to the captive in earlier official documents always refer to him as simply 'the prisoner'.

Visitors who had seen him alive had always witnessed him with his face covered, but the prisoner did not always wear an iron mask. It was in place only when there was any chance that he might encounter members of the public; otherwise his mask was of black velvet, and in the security of his cell the prisoner often wore no mask at all, a practical necessity if he was to eat and breathe normally. It is clear that the unauthorised removal of the mask meant instant death for the prisoner. But why wear a mask at all? Since the wearing of the mask was apparently by royal order and not by the prisoner's choice, such things as severe disfigurement by wounds or disease can be ruled out. Was the order a royal quirk or an odd punishment? Both seem unlikely, and neither is in keeping with Louis XIV's usual judicial decisions. So the mask was intended to keep the identity of the prisoner secret and that rules out most of the official and noble possibilities for the man's identity.

Rumours abounded. One had it that the masked man was the playwright Molière. He had quarrelled with Louis XIV and was briefly imprisoned, but he had been reconciled with Louis and his death had been widely reported. Another rumour hinted that the prisoner was an English noble, but there were no contemporary reports of such a man mysteriously disappearing and ending up in the dungeons of a French prison. A more likely candidate was Ercole Antonio Matteoli (Marchioly?) who had secretly alerted France's enemies of Louis's plans to buy the Italian border fortress of Casale. In his anger Louis had Matteoli kidnapped in 1679 and taken to Pinerolo, but Saint-Mars reported the death of the only prisoner in his charge with a personal servant in 1681, and Matteoli had been attended in Pinerolo by a servant. Some averred that the masked prisoner was Fouquet, Louis XIV's larcenous finance minister who had been sentenced to life imprisonment in 1661. Although it was reported that Fouquet had died in Pinerolo in 1680, his death actually occurred in 1687 and was kept secret. Even so, it was too early to be reconciled with later reported sightings of the man in the iron mask.

A more likely candidate was Eustache Dauger (or Danger) who, although believed by the credulous to be Louis XIV's twin, was briefly Fouquet's valet. He certainly wore a black velvet mask when travelling from fortress to fortress and when members of the public were in the grounds of the Bastille. Why is not clear. That his identity should be concealed from the public by a face mask seems strange when he was only a valet. Did he resemble someone of importance? In fact, although he had been commandeered into service as one of Fouquet's valets, he was, under his real name of Etienne Martin, a dangerous agent who had become involved in the French royal court's poison scandal, and thus was important enough to warrant an iron mask.

The rumours of the masked man's supposed royal blood are more fanciful, but they give the wearing of the mask some semblance of purpose. It was widely rumoured that Louis XIV was one of identical twins, the elder of whom died soon after birth. This gave rise to the assertion that the prisoner was indeed the twin brother who had survived, had been brought up abroad, and had returned to claim his inheritance. If the twins were identical, the older one's resemblance to Louis XIV would have been so striking as to make imprisonment and a mask sensible precautions. But such a secret would be difficult to preserve, and doctors, midwives and those associated with the twin's upbringing abroad would have had to have been silenced or suborned. The same problem relates to the more fanciful suggestion that the prisoner was Louis XIV's half-brother, son of his mother Anne of Austria and Cardinal Mazarin, who was Chief Minister Richelieu's successor. That the queen and the cardinal were very close is beyond dispute, but there is no specific evidence to suggest a sexual liaison, and Mazarin would have been most unlikely to place his position in Church and State in jeopardy by pursuing one.

Interesting, and possibly even more fanciful, is the suggestion that the man in the iron mask was Louis XIV's father. Anne of Austria and Louis XIII had been married for thirteen years without children when the queen became pregnant in 1638. King and queen had been going their separate ways and largely living apart for some years. Possibly to allay suspicion, the story of the conception – how Louis had gone to a convent gate to gawp at one of the nuns, got trapped in a thunderstorm, and ended up in the queen's bed in her nearby château where he had taken refuge – was widely disseminated at the time. But it is conceivable that the consumptive Louis XIII alarmed Richelieu by failing to sire an heir, and that Richelieu had procured for Anne a handsome scion of the House of Bourbon, telling her that it was her duty both to the State and to Louis. The father would have been persuaded to live abroad, but if he returned and bore a remarkable resemblance to his son, then security would demand his faceless detention. It would have been easy for Louis to dispose of the prisoner, yet surely even he would have baulked at killing his own father. But all this depends on a supposition of Louis XIII's impotence. In fact, the queen had already had pregnancies that did not run to term, and she did give birth to a second son, Philippe, in 1640. For Richelieu to have provided the queen with one partner would have been risky; for him to have provided her with a string of them would have been foolhardy, and he was too wily for that. Of course Anne of Austria might well have been promiscuous on her own account. This was certainly rumoured, and her flirtation with the Duke of Buckingham had caused a sensation in 1625.

So we are left with the conclusion that there is no certainty about the identity of the man in the mask. None of those who knew it left any written identification of him, and Louis XIV barred any discussion of the subject. Until recently the most likely candidate – mainly because of the want of any other – was Eustache Dauger. The more fanciful candidates do not bear close scrutiny, but there is still the unanswered question as to why, if indeed the prisoner was Fouquet's valet, he was forced to wear a mask. He was certainly of too low birth for him to bear a dangerous resemblance to anyone of importance, and he was too obscure for anyone to recognise him. Until a more satisfactory answer could be offered, there was still room for other candidates.

The most convincing identification came in 2005 in Roger Macdonald's book, *The Man in the Iron Mask*. He argues that the prisoner was in fact Charles de Batz D'Artagnan, captain of the First Company of Musketeers. D'Artagnan was a brilliant swordsman and a notorious womaniser; tall and handsome, he regarded all married women of charm as fair game. He had guarded Nicholas Fouquet, Louis XIV's disgraced finance minister, during his lengthy trial; he moved easily in court circles; and, of course, he collected a great deal of information through pillow talk. His close association with Fouquet made Louis's chief minister, Colbert, suspicious of him. He managed to quarrel with Vauban, Louis's chief engineer and the apple of the king's eye, and in 1672 he became embroiled in a dispute with Louvois, the war minister. D'Artagnan knew some members of the court had engaged in black masses and others in financial speculation; he had learned embarrassing personal details about many prominent individuals, such as widow Scarron's disreputable youth, no matter how much she now claimed to be pious and virtuous – she was, as Madame de Maintenon, later to become Louis XIV's mistress and wife. Louis expected those who served him to be both obsequious and obedient. D'Artagnan was neither, and he was impervious to the king's reprimands. It must have been with relief that Louis and Louvois decided to offer D'Artagnan, now fifty years old, a chance of death and glory. In 1673 the First Musketeers were thrown into the siege of Maestricht where casualties were predicted to be extremely heavy; Louis and Louvois thought D'Artagnan would almost certainly be killed leading his men.

But things did not turn out quite as planned. As expected, unlike the vast majority of commanders, D'Artagnan led his men from the front and fell severely wounded. He was not gathered up with the wounded and was reported as dead. When he was found several hours later he fell into the hands of Louvois, and with only a very few people in the know, and certainly not Louis, he was conveyed to the Bastille. Louvois might have had D'Artagnan despatched there and then, but was concerned that news of it might leak out. More importantly he did not know how much damaging information D'Artagnan had passed on to others and he wanted to find out. The governor of the Bastille, François Besmaux, had been an enemy of D'Artagnan since early musketeer days, and he was also a connoisseur of masks. Instructed that no one must recognise D'Artagnan, he had a steel mask forged for him as a measure of his revenge.

But rumours began to circulate about the mysterious prisoner in the Bastille. Afraid that the truth might emerge, and that the king, who had been kept in the dark, would be enraged, Louvois decided to move the prisoner to the remote Alpine fortress of Pinerolo. This meant entrusting D'Artagnan to Fouquet's jailer, Saint-Mars, who was under the impression that he was indebted to D'Artagnan for some early favour. He therefore felt it his duty not only to guard his new prisoner, but also to protect him. While D'Artagnan lived, Saint-Mars could enjoy a salary and expenses for looking after an important prisoner. If D'Artagnan were to die then the income would cease and Saint-Mars would have little reason to keep quiet. All the while Louis was unaware of the prisoner's identity, but as years went by it became difficult for people to believe that he had not had a hand in the affair.

The king was eventually informed of the truth by Louvois in 1691. Louvois hoped that by threatening to reveal it to the public he could retain his waning influence with the king. But Louvois died shortly afterwards, and Louis apparently decided that disclosure some eighteen years after the event would be damaging to him personally. Moreover, to release D'Artagnan now could well lead to his incautiously spreading stories about Madame de Maintenon. So D'Artagnan was left in Saint-Mars's care, moving from prison to prison, and eventually to the Bastille. Saint-Mars treated him kindly, but from 1703 he was subjected to a more rigid regime. Then Saint-Mars, absent from the Bastille briefly on family matters, was told on his return that D'Artagnan was dead. He had simply been moved to another part of the Bastille which the aged Saint-Mars never visited. D'Artagnan is believed to have died in 1711 aged eighty-eight, abandoned and forgotten.

This account is backed by references to all the available sources, including Saint-Mars's incautious and revealing remark that 'All the people that the public believe to be dead are not.' It seems that in the absence of any source that specifically identifies him, D'Artagnan is by far the likeliest to have been the man in the iron mask. But perhaps not everyone will be convinced.

HOW DID COLONEL BLOOD GET AWAY
WITH HIS LIFE?

Everybody has heard of the exploits of Thomas Blood, the bold adventurer who broke into the Tower of London in 1671 and stole the crown jewels. What is less well known is what happened to him afterwards, and in particular why Blood's fate was not different.

Blood was born in Ireland in or about 1618, a son in a minor line of would-be gentry, who had ideas of magnifying the family's modest fortunes through opportunism and adventure. In the sixteenth century he would have been a buccaneer or an explorer, and would perhaps have emulated the West Indian feats of Henry Morgan at Maracaibo or Francis Drake off Porto Bello. Because of the way things stood in the reign of Charles I, he attempted to increase his fortune by feats of arms.

He took the side of Parliament in the Civil War of the 1640s, and rose to the rank of colonel in the Cromwellian army. History does not relate what Colonel Blood thought of the bloody and brutal conquest of Ireland in 1649, but there is no evidence that as an Irish Protestant (which he claimed to be) he showed even a flicker of remorse. However, with the restoration of Charles II in 1660 he was deprived of his estates and reduced to idleness and poverty. So it was that in 1663 he put himself at the head of a plot to seize Dublin Castle – the centre of English administration in Ireland – and to capture and kill the Duke of Ormonde, the English Lord Lieutenant. When the plot was discovered Blood's chief accomplices were arrested, brought to trial and executed, though he himself made good his escape to the Low Countries, which at the time were conducting a series of trade wars with the government in London. After his return to England in 1670 he became party to a number of insurrections in England and Scotland. However, the ballads sung about him, and the recollections of those who were acquainted with him, do not depict him as a lovable and raffish rascal who stirred the popular imagination, but rather as a dangerous terrorist and hired assassin. In December 1670, for example, he renewed his hostility towards the Duke of Ormonde, at that time resident in England. With a gang of hired ruffians he attempted to kidnap and even to hang the duke; it was only the intervention of Ormonde's servants that prevented the design from being carried out. Once again, Blood made good his escape.

In 1671 he embarked upon his most sensational and dangerous scheme – that of stealing the crown jewels. One day in the spring of that year Talbot Edwards, the elderly deputy keeper of the Tower of London, was taking tea with his wife when a clergyman and his wife knocked on the door and asked whether they might be allowed to see the crown jewels. Before the days of organised tourism this was not an unusual request. Edwards was not slow in conducting them to the room in which the jewels were stored and parading his small stock of learning on the subject of the royal sceptre, the sword of state, the bejewelled coronets and gauntlets and – in pride of place – the crown imperial, used at coronations. The visitors were duly impressed with their visit, and the parson called only a week later to present the deputy keeper with a pair of gloves for Mrs Edwards 'in gratitude for her kindness'.

It seemed perfectly natural that their clergyman friend should appear once again, this time on the morning of 9 May, with two strangers, visitors to London, so that they could view the royal regalia.

This time, however, things turned out differently. As he was giving his usual spiel, Edwards found himself pinioned by the visitors, a cloak thrown over his head and a bung thrust into his mouth to stifle his cries. Though he was over eighty years old, he was highly incensed and struggled violently. His assailants renewed their efforts, striking him repeatedly with a wooden mallet they had brought with them, and when this was not enough they stabbed the old man with a dagger. Then the reckless trio set about stowing their booty. Blood knelt and beat the crown out of shape with his mallet, scattering jewels over the floor, then hid it under his cloak. Meanwhile, one of his accomplices tried to push the sceptre down his baggy breeches. Finding it too long, he started hastily filing it in half to make it more portable. Then their lookout on the floor below whistled a warning. Edwards's son and son-in-law were coming up the stairs to pay the couple a visit.

The thieves fled with their trophies, bumping roughly into the visitors on the stairs and pushing past them. The cry of 'Stop thief!' went up, and the warder on duty at the drawbridge was alerted. Blood fired his pistol at him and he fell, though not seriously hurt. Edwards's son threw himself across the drawbridge after his father's attackers, and as they tried to mount their horses tethered nearby, with the help of enthusiastic by-standers he managed to overpower them.

Though forced to submit to this citizens' arrest, Blood haughtily refused to give an account of himself, demanding instead an audience with the king.

Astonishingly, this was granted. Far from throwing himself on Charles's mercy, Blood uttered a tirade of self-justification, regretting not only his failure to lift the royal treasure: he quoted an earlier occasion when he had had the king in his pistol sights as he went down to the river at Battersea to bathe, but had failed to shoot him. He had, he said, been deterred from the intended assassination by an 'awe of majesty' which prevented him from killing – though apparently not from robbing – Charles. The king made no comment on this extraordinary outburst but remanded Blood to the Tower pending sentence. When it was delivered this sentence was even more astonishing than the circumstances leading to it. Charles II freed Blood with a royal pardon. More than that, the king restored Blood's estates in Ireland to him and awarded him a pension of £500 a year, which he drew every year until his death in 1680. Talbot Edwards, who survived the knife attack, and his family got no reward at all for their gallant defence of the king's treasure. London was aghast with incredulity.

A number of explanations have been offered for King Charles's extraordinary behaviour, though none can be accepted unequivocally. Was it merely a royal whim? Charles was well known for his unpredictable behaviour and he liked to keep his courtiers on the hop by acting on a momentary caprice, but such a neglect of his own security makes this explanation unlikely. Was there some deeper understanding between Charles and Blood? The idea that Blood had earlier performed some action on the king's behalf so murderous and wicked that he could now call in his favour and name his recompense has been put forward. This is also unlikely, since obviously the best way to silence Blood would have been to kill him while the chance presented itself. Did the king prefer to go on holding Blood as a sort of trump card in case he should ever need the services of a reckless and courageous servant who would do his bidding with no questions asked? Perhaps.

In the end the most likely explanation for Blood's apparent immunity from the law is the simplest and stems from his powerful friends. Blood's protector and patron was George Villiers, Duke of Buckingham, who was the declared enemy of Ormonde. It is possible, though not likely, that Buckingham had been behind Blood's attacks on the duke. Buckingham was one of the king's principal ministers and a member of the so-called Cabal who managed the Cavalier Parliament and helped to direct Charles's policies. In addition he was also the close companion and favourite of Charles II, and it is quite possible that it was he who intervened with the king on Blood's behalf to save the ruffian's life.

WHO WAS THE FAMOUS HIGHWAYMAN DICK TURPIN?

The story is widely told of Richard ('Dick') Turpin, an intrepid highwayman working as head of a gang of notorious cut-throats based in Epping Forest, Essex. He fled northwards with a price of £100 on his head after killing a man and, after a historic ride on his famous mare Black Bess, reached York overnight, where he was discovered, arrested, tried and later hanged in 1739. To generations his has seemed a very bold and dramatic career. However, this story is false in almost every particular. How

*did this fictitious version of events come into
existence, and why does it continue to be preferred
to the truth?*

In fact Dick Turpin, born in 1706, was trained as a
butcher, which helped him when he became a cattle-
thief – he knew how to joint and carve up an animal
and he knew which cuts of meat his customers would
prefer. He graduated from rustling cattle to stealing
horses, and after that became a highwayman. It was in
connection with horse stealing and highway robbery
that a price was placed on his head in 1737. Shortly
after, he shot and killed his partner, Tom King, by
mistake while trying to evade capture. It was at this
point that he fled Essex and headed north for safety.

He did not reach York overnight, but instead spent
several months on the journey. He stopped off first at
Long Sutton in Lincolnshire where he stole more
horses, but he escaped from the constable who was
taking him before the magistrate and fled to Welton in
Yorkshire. There he took the name of John Palmer and
assumed the character of a gentleman, but he continued to steal horses in numerous trips to Lincolnshire, disposing of his gains by sale or exchange back
in Yorkshire. Having shot a cock belonging to his
landlord in 1739, he was brought before the quarter
sessions at Beverley. Enquiry was made in Lincolnshire
about the sources of his income and the magistrates
there replied that John Palmer was well known in the
county, not as a gentleman but as a sheep rustler and
horse thief who had eluded arrest and absconded.

In the light of this knowledge it was considered wise
to transfer Turpin to York Castle, where he was held for
some months. During this time he wrote a letter to his

brother in Essex, asking him for a character reference to stand him in good stead during his forthcoming trial. His brother, however, refused to pay the postage on the letter and it passed into the hands of Turpin's old schoolmaster who, having taught Turpin to write, knew his handwriting. The Essex magistrates sent the schoolmaster to York to provide evidence of identification. In due course Turpin was convicted and sentenced to hang. Though he made repeated efforts to get local bigwigs to intercede on his behalf, no one spoke in his favour.

As the day of his execution drew near he bought himself a new coat and a pair of pumps, and hired five men at 10s each to follow his cart to the gallows as mourners. On the day of his execution he bowed graciously to the spectators who had come to witness the event, spoke for nearly half an hour with his executioner 'with astonishing indifference and intrepidity', and finally threw himself off the ladder up to the scaffold and perished in a few minutes.

His body was brought to the Blue Boar in Castle Gate where it was exhibited to the public. Afterwards it was buried in a specially deep grave in the churchyard close by. Even so, the body was stolen overnight and was afterwards found in a garden belonging to one of the surgeons of the city. It was restored to the burial place, the coffin this time filled with quicklime.

It remains something of a mystery why the fictitious account of Turpin's life took precedence over the dramatic details of the true story. How did the fictitious version gain credence? It began probably as an error on the part of the nineteenth-century novelist, William Harrison Ainsworth, who also mythologised the career of a late eighteenth-century housebreaker by

the name of Jack Shepherd. Ainsworth either deliberately or accidentally conflated Dick Turpin's ride
with that of another famous horseman, Swift Nick,
who rode from London to York in 1676 in order to
provide himself with an alibi for a crime he had
committed. It was Nick's horse, not Dick's, who was
known as Black Bess. The popularity of Dick Turpin
rested chiefly on the thrilling achievement of that
night ride, and as such he became a main staple of
bedtime stories for generations of small boys. His name
became legendary, especially among gypsies, who in
the nineteenth century frequently named their boy-
children Dick in his honour.

WHO WERE TOM, DICK AND HARRY?

In Brewer's Dictionary of Phrase and Fable *the
phrase 'Tom, Dick and Harry' is said to be a
Victorian term for 'the man in the street',
especially for people of little note. The same
source goes on to quote 'Brown, Jones and
Robinson' as the term for the vulgar rich who try to
give themselves airs. However, there is some
reason to believe that Tom, Dick and Harry were
real people.*

The phrase appears to be the equivalent of the
American expression for an unknown person, 'John
Doe' (or, in the case of a female, 'Jane Doe'). The use of
the names goes back a long way. Indeed, the phrase was
recorded as early as 1734. Even earlier, Shakespeare
used the names 'Tom, Dick and Francis' in his play
Henry IV, Part I in just the same kind of context.

However, the author Joan Moody in *Burford's Roads, Part Two: Vagabonds, Villains and Highwaymen* says that the names have a genuine historical connection with the late eighteenth-century Home Counties. She claims to have evidence that they refer to the three brothers Tom, Dick and Harry Dunsden, whose exploits on the Oxfordshire–Gloucestershire border gave them popular notoriety in the 1770s. Perhaps it was because no one could locate them definitely, and because of the difficulty of properly attributing the blame for their misdeeds, that Tom, Dick and Harry came to acquire their present context of anonymity.

Tom was the first to die, in an encounter with the local constabulary, but Dick and Harry Dunsden were seized a little later after a wild night of drink and gambling with their friends. They were tried and executed in Gloucester in 1784. After their hanging, their bodies were brought by horse and cart across the Cotswolds to Capps Lodge on the Downs, and there they were hung in chains on an oak known as the gibbet tree. During that summer many curious visitors came to see them, and it was only in the autumn of 1784 that the two corpses were taken down to be buried. The chains that bound them were not removed and remained on the tree as late as the 1930s.

WHAT HAPPENED TO 'POOR FRED'?

Frederick Louis, Prince of Wales, eldest son of King George II, has generally received a bad press from historians. Only one biographer, Sir George Young, has attempted any kind of reappraisal of his character which for 250 years has suffered very largely at the hands of the letters of Horace Walpole and the memoirs of Lord Hervey. They paint a picture of an unintelligent boor dabbling in politics that was beyond his understanding, lacking social graces and treating his parents with rudeness and contempt. It was in the mysterious manner of the prince's death that his career reached its dramatic climax.

Frederick was born in 1707 and was kept out of England during the reign of his grandfather, George I. George wanted Frederick to be educated in Hanover, and was concerned that at least one senior member of the family should remain there so that Hanover – of which George, as Elector, was still ruler – should not feel neglected. When he arrived in England in 1728 Frederick was already at odds with his parents. His father, now King George II, had made tentative plans when he was Prince of Wales to exclude Frederick from the succession in favour of his younger brother William, later Duke of Cumberland. George II's animosity showed further when, despite Parliament's grant of an extra £100,000 per annum in the Civil List to cater for Frederick, the king saw to it that he was granted only £50,000.

It was nothing unusual in Hanoverian history for the monarch and the heir to the throne to be at odds. Both George II and Queen Caroline were understandably concerned that the popularity of the young prince could easily exceed theirs. They did their best, therefore, to belittle and humiliate him. Caroline referred publicly to her son in terms which were so vindictive and vituperative that they were a disgrace to motherhood and an embarrassment to all who heard them: 'ungrateful viper' was one of her less outrageous descriptions of him. Horace Walpole, youngest son of George's long-serving prime minister, encouraged scurrilous literary tittle-tattle about the prince, often by anonymous authors and poets. Frederick responded by becoming the hope of the opposition to Walpole – a ragbag of Tories and disaffected Whigs. This opposition was to become more formidable with the formation of the Boy Patriots – young members of Parliament whose ranks were swelled in 1735 by the election of William Pitt (the Elder) as MP for Old Sarum. Frederick now posed an even greater threat to Walpole and his fellow ministers, and his home at Leicester House became the headquarters of a growing and more powerful opposition. In alarm Walpole attempted to repair the breach between Frederick and his father, but to no avail. In 1737 Frederick insisted on removing his wife Augusta from Hampton Court because he did not want his heir to be born under his parents' roof. Although Augusta was in significant discomfort and in the early stages of labour, her coach rattled furiously over the rutted roads and cobbled streets the considerable distance to St James's Palace. George was enraged. Frederick was banned from court, and the hostility intensified.

London was enthralled by the growing rift because it took practical form in the development of musical rivalry. George was a patron of Handel. Frederick encouraged Handel's rivals. These musicians were so devoid of talent as to be almost forgotten today, but Frederick did succeed in rousing the mob against Handel's operas and in ensuring the success of Gay's *Beggar's Opera*. Handel thought it prudent to repair his own breach with the prince by composing a marriage anthem for him in 1736. The king did not forgive Handel for this insult until the composer commemorated in music George's (exaggerated) contribution to the battle of Dettingen in 1743.

Frederick may not have had much taste in music, but he was a great patron of art, despite his straitened finances. His thrifty and well-chosen purchases were to form the nucleus of the magnificent royal art collection which his son was to assemble after his accession to the throne as George III in 1760. Frederick was able to step up his artistic acquisitions in 1745 when the Pelham ministry persuaded George to allow his son the sum originally intended to maintain the Prince of Wales in proper style. George was very grudging about this but Pelham thought it wise, in view of George II's advancing years, to offer an olive branch to the prince.

Even so, the sparring and back-biting in the royal family continued. Frederick had not forgotten that his younger brother William had long been the favourite. After William, Duke of Cumberland, suppressed the Scots at Culloden in 1746, Frederick circulated stories, most of which had some elements of truth, about the massacres and crimes committed by William's officers and men in Scotland. Cumberland was never able to live down the reputation of butcher which his brother was delighted to canvass for him. But Frederick had behaved himself during the Jacobite rebellion and had been rewarded with an increase in his allowance.

When political fighting resumed after the Jacobite scare had died down, Frederick was so confident of the success of the opposition, either during his father's lifetime or certainly upon his demise, that he began selecting ministers for the takeover. His choices were not always sensible or wise; they included the sycophant Bubb Dodington, who had little in the way of talent and was an easy butt for Horace Walpole's ridicule. Frederick had few political aims other than to remove his father's ministers and give power to his own nominees, but he was said by his enemies to have derived his political opinions from *Idea of a Patriot King* by Viscount Bolingbroke, which was full of outdated ideas even though it was written in 1738. It was almost commonplace in the eighteenth century to accuse opponents of the Whig oligarchy of being unduly influenced by Bolingbroke's work, and Frederick's son George III was later to be tarred with this same brush by those who accused him of aiming at an absolute monarchy.

Although the Pelham ministry seemed to go from strength to strength, by 1751 Frederick felt that he would not have long to wait to exercise power. The House of Hanover was not noted for longevity, and Frederick's grandfather George I had died at sixty-seven, exactly the age that George II had now reached. But then on 20 March Frederick, who had been suffering from pleurisy, had a particularly severe bout of coughing. As it eased he suddenly exclaimed 'Je sens la mort', collapsed into a servant's arms and died almost instantly. The cause of death was never clearly established. Some attributed it to the abscess that plagued him after he had been struck by a cricket ball, but abscesses do not normally cause such a sudden death, neither does pleurisy. A stroke or heart attack were strong contenders, but would they have been accompanied by the premonition he so clearly expressed? Another possibility is viral pneumonia, a tragic and sudden affliction of the lungs which has been known to strike down apparently healthy victims in a matter of seconds. Whatever the cause of death, it was beyond the skill of eighteenth-century pathology to determine.

Decorum did not deter the Whig establishment from delighting in Frederick's demise. Horace Walpole carefully preserved the doggerel that has for so long served as Frederick's epitaph:

> Here lies Fred,
> Who was alive, and is dead;
> Had it been his father,
> I had much rather;
> Had it been his brother,
> Still better than another;
> Had it been his sister,
> No one would have missed her;
> Had it been the whole generation
> Still better for the nation;
> But since 'tis only Fred
> Who was alive and is dead –
> There's no more to be said.

Here the irreverence extended to both sides in the political quarrel, and it was well that the author remained anonymous.

The widowed Augusta had no choice but to throw herself and her son George on the mercy of the choleric old king, and the royal rift was to a large extent healed. But George did not entirely forgive. He hated Pitt and did his best to keep him out of office, even to the extent of refusing to reprieve Admiral Byng, shot to cover up the mistakes of others, in order to deflect criticism from the ministry. But Frederick's death merely delayed, and did not prevent, the rise of Pitt. Although the prince's sudden demise ended the disgraceful rift between monarch and heir, the quarrel was to be repeated in the reign of Frederick's son George III, whose feud with his own eldest son was notorious.

Frederick's talents have been obscured by his enemies' propaganda, and his faults magnified by those determined to deny him a reputation. His premature demise was certainly a relief to the government and a blow to the opposition, but that he died of natural causes has never been questioned, even though no satisfactory explanation of his death is ever likely to be offered.

WHO WERE SNOW WHITE AND THE SEVEN SHORT MINERS?

The Brothers Grimm are famously reputed for writing fairy tales and for inventing the modern German language. Neither facet of their reputation is entirely true. The elder of the two, Jacob Ludwig (1785–1863), traced the mutations of German consonants in his Deutsche Grammatik; *he also tried to construct a more scientific basis for the language and to formulate into laws its hazy grammar conventions. In collaboration with his younger brother Wilhelm Carl (1786–1859) he was the author of a series of books on mythology and folklore, studying the facts and legends of the German people's history. From these the two distilled their famous stories, published between 1812 and 1815 under the title* Kinder- und

Hausmärchen (Children's and Household Tales),
and translated into English in 1823 by George
Cruikshank. But were they in fact fairy tales?

Modern literary research has suggested that the story
of *Snow White and the Seven Dwarfs* is not entirely
fiction, but is based on real people and real places in
quite recent times. The place was the drowsy
settlement of Lohr on the River Main, not far from
Frankfurt, which was in the eighteenth century a
bustling town. There were mines nearby in the seven
mountains close to the village of Bieber, at that time a
prolific producer of copper and silver. The heroine of
the story was not a poor mistreated princess with a
weakness for tiny folk; she was instead Maria Sophia
Margaretha Catherina von Erthal, daughter of the local
prince, Philipp Christoph, Lord of Rieneck. She was
born in 1729 and grew up in Rieneck Castle with her
father and his second wife, Claudia Elisabeth von
Erthal. One of the rooms of the castle still contains a
'talking' mirror, an acoustic toy the like of which was
very fashionable in the eighteenth century. This was
made locally in Lohr, a town renowned at that time for
its craft work and for the quality of the looking glasses
it produced.

There seems to be no basis for the view that Claudia
Elisabeth was wicked as a stepmother, but the young
Maria Sophia generated considerable sympathy among
the townsfolk on account of her uncertain health. As a
child she suffered from smallpox and this left her
partially blind. She had, however, a sweet and agree-
able nature and put up with her disability without
complaint. Nor is it clear why she left home in the way
she did. However, it is perfectly possible that people

like the dwarfs actually existed. The mines at Bieber were extremely cramped, their tunnels accessible only to the shortest of miners, and it is believed that these workers often wore brightly coloured caps or hoods, supposedly to give them protection against bumping their heads. But how and why Maria Sophia took up residence with these miners is not known.

The detail of the princess being offered a poisoned apple does not occur in all versions of the story, but it may be linked to an occasion when someone recovered after previously appearing to die. As for the legend of the glass coffin, such a thing was not at all unusual. They can still be found, especially in Catholic churches, where they are used to display holy relics – or even bodies, especially when the dead person is a beautiful young woman.

Of course, this version of the 'real' Snow White is not universally accepted. Some regard it as an elaborate joke, dreamed up in a boozy German beer-cellar. For every scholar who believes that the story of Snow White is based on fact, there is another who says that similar tales exist in all cultures throughout the world, and that they borrow heavily from one another in the details with which they are furnished. The archetype of the older woman competing with a younger for the attention of a man is almost universal, and the romantic detail of the coffin and the poisoned apple are repeated in many different situations. Wicked stepmothers occur again and again in fairy stories – for example, there is one in *Cinderella*. Such thinking tends to disprove the theory of a particular origin for any individual story. Marina Warner, an expert on the origins of fairy tales, says: 'It's an organic business. Stories grow branches; they creep across cultures and nations.' So perhaps Snow White is no more than a fairy tale after all.

CASSIDY AND SUNDANCE: KNIGHTS OR CRIMINALS?

In the late 1960s a very successful film called Butch Cassidy and the Sundance Kid *was made in Hollywood. It presented the lives of the two outlaws in the vein of a comedy-thriller. In point of fact their real lives were sad, confusing and rather sordid, lacking the glamour with which legend has invested them. In particular, their end, though dramatic and gruesome, was not nearly so clear-cut as the film made out. To this day, the fate of both men remains shrouded in apparently quite impenetrable mystery.*

Butch Cassidy was born Robert LeRoy Parker in southern Utah in 1866, eldest of fourteen children. His Mormon family had left the mills of Lancashire ten years earlier as the result of a Mormon sweep of England for converts in the previous year. He grew into a generous youth, good with children and with a likeable grin; it was his boast, until his very last days, that he had never killed a man. He was good with cattle and with horses and worked as a farm-hand, a cowboy and a horse dealer. He loved horses: he bred them, broke them, trained them, raced them – and from time to time stole them, or used them to escape with other people's money. He collected aliases with equal enthusiasm. From time to time he called himself James Ryan, Bob Place, Jim Lowe and, in South

America, Santiago Maxwell, but the name he seemed to favour most was Butch Cassidy – the Cassidy from a childhood friend whom he much admired, and the Butch because of his skill with a meat cleaver on rustled cattle which he disposed of to butchers. His first brush with the law came over his breaking into the local general store and stealing a pair of overalls, but he soon found that his bad reputation as a no-good and a horse thief preceded him wherever he went. He was frequently in bad company, and in 1894 was sent to Wyoming State Penitentiary for two years for cattle-rustling. Later he was involved in, or was said to have been involved in, numerous bank robberies, where his skills in preparing relays of horses and supplies for his getaway were legendary, and also in armed robberies of railroad trains transporting gold, silver and paper money, chiefly as payrolls for company employees. The two safe havens where he had loyal friends and to which he frequently returned were the Robbers' Roost country in southern Utah, and the Hole-in-the-Wall maze of dried-up gulches and canyons in Wyoming. This was the hideout of the Wild Bunch, as they were known.

The Sundance Kid was really Harry Alonzo Longabaugh, born to a devout Baptist family in Phoenixville, near Philadelphia, in 1867. By the age of thirteen, he was working as a farm-hand in Pennsylvania within 10 miles of his home, but in 1882, caught up in the craze to 'Go West, young man!', he moved with his family to Durango in south-western Colorado to establish a homestead and raise horses. In 1885 the family moved 50 miles further west to Montezuma County, and though he was only seventeen, Harry moved on to become a cattle herdsman near Springer in New Mexico. He took a number of different cattle jobs over the next few years in both New Mexico and Colorado, and found himself caught up not only in the severe drought which afflicted the area in 1886 but also in the great blizzard of 1887. His ill fortune drove him in the direction of petty criminality: in Wyoming he stole a horse, a saddle and a bridle from one of his cowboy friends and a revolver from another. He was arrested, tried and sentenced to eighteen months with hard labour, not in Joliet Penitentiary, Illinois, where he would have expected to go with such a sentence, but to the newly built jail at Sundance, Wyoming. Here, still not yet twenty years old, he was the youngest prisoner doing time. So he became the 'Sundance Kid' and not the 'Joliet Kid'. The prison authorities considered him a slippery customer because he made several attempts to escape; as a result he served the whole of his sentence without remission for good conduct. On his release he went to Canada and found work near Calgary, but he could not keep out of trouble there either, and in 1892 he drifted south to Montana. He successfully robbed a train at Malta, Montana, in the autumn of 1892, though his haul of booty was meagre. There is no evidence that he ever met Butch Cassidy before 1896, but both had had considerable experience of cattle-rustling and armed robbery independently before then. The two became partners as members of the Wild Bunch in Wyoming in 1896.

Their career together, from 1897 to 1908, was brief but spectacular. In 1897 they pulled off robberies at Fort Bridger of a post-office-cum-saloon, and at Belle Fourche, South Dakota, of the Butte County Bank, where they carried off thousands of dollars in gold and notes. They robbed another train at Wilcox, Wyoming, in 1899 using dynamite to blast open the safes in the express car and making off with company payrolls. They looted $55,000 from a Union Pacific express at Tipton, Wyoming, a few months later, and in 1900 robbed the First National Bank of Winnemucca, Nevada, where they emptied the vaults of notes and coins, carrying them off in ore sacks they had brought with them. In between these exploits they considered volunteering for military service in the Spanish-American War of 1898, and Butch Cassidy actually watched a body being interred under his own name at a place called Price, not far from Robbers' Roost, commenting 'it would be a good idea to attend his own funeral just once in a lifetime'.

Generally, however, it proved easier to turn towards a life of crime than away from it, and by 1900 things in the Mid-West were getting a little too hot for them. The Pinkerton Detective Agency was hot on their tracks, and one operator, Charles Siringo, was proving particularly shrewd and tenacious in his pursuit of them. So Cassidy and the Kid decided to pull out and go where the grass was greener. Somewhere in South America seemed a good idea. They took with them their chief female companion, Etha, or Etta, Place (an abbreviation for 'Ethel' — if that was her real name), who had accompanied them for some time in their Mid-Western exploits. The trio went to Buffalo and then on to New York, where they saw the sights for several weeks before taking a ship to Buenos Aires. Though Cassidy and Sundance were accused of being involved in later bank robberies at Wagner, Montana, in 1901 and at Dupont, Illinois, in 1902, such charges will not stick since it seems likely that by that time both men were out of the country.

The fact that the men were reasonably intelligent and unafraid of hard work is shown by their fortunes in the Argentine. They took a considerable spread of land in western Chubut province and for several years worked it successfully in ranching cattle and raising horses. Both men were occasionally homesick for the United States and took trips back to the East Coast and the West Coast. On the last occasion Etta went into hospital for an operation and never went back to Argentina. After they sold out their cattle interest, the pair also worked for a mining company, where they enjoyed the reputation of being honest and industrious employees; but somehow they could not keep away from criminal activity, however hard they tried.

In 1905 they were suspected of being involved in the robbery of the Banco de Tarapacá at Rio Gallegos, where they were said to have lifted cash and silver of about $100,000 in value; and later in the same year they were said to have stolen almost $140,000 from the Banco de la Nación at Villa Mercedes. After a smaller raid in November 1908 at Huaca Huañusca (south of Quechisla, Bolivia) in which they stole a mining company payroll worth only a few thousand dollars, they were unlucky to be cornered a few miles away at San Vicente by armed police reinforced by a passing Bolivian military patrol. In a shoot-out both suffered multiple bullet wounds and were killed. The bodies were buried nearby shortly afterwards in a native Indian graveyard.

At least, that was the commonly accepted story. In fact it was doubtful whether the two men killed at

San Vicente were Cassidy and the Kid. In 1970, in the course of investigations, the two bodies were exhumed from their graves, and it was shown that there must have been some mistake. Doubts were complicated by the fact that there had been multiple burials in the same plot, as a result of which it was impossible to identify the remains with any certainty. What was originally thought to have been Cassidy's skull turned out to be that of a native Indian, while other bones believed to have been those of the Kid produced negative results when DNA comparisons were made with surviving members of the Longabaugh family. There was even doubt as to whether the grave that had been excavated was the right one.

Finding a final solution to the problem of the men's fate proved to be even more difficult than this. There turned out to be numerous uncorroborated sightings of Butch in the years after 1908: like the equally famous Elvis Presley, it seemed impossible for him to stay dead. He was seen at railway stations, in saloons, in hotels and driving cars in town and countryside in a number of US states. Then Cassidy's surviving sister wrote a book in 1975 in which she made the astonishing claim that Butch had driven up to the family ranch in 1925 saying that he was mystified by the reports of his death in South America and explaining that he had met up with the Kid and Etta Place in Mexico City, then travelled in Europe before settling in the American north-west. He said he had been too ashamed of his lurid past to return sooner. According to this sister, Cassidy died of pneumonia in 1937 at the age of seventy-one. The only trouble was that the remainder of the family did not bear out her version of events – and in any case she kept changing her story, elaborating the detail and altering basic facts as the years passed.

The final complication in the search for the truth was that there was another, quite different version of Cassidy's story. It suggested that in later years he had assumed yet another alias, calling himself William T. Phillips, and had lived in Seattle. However, at a later date Phillips's widow confessed that such a man had existed, but that he was someone acquainted with Cassidy who merely impersonated him. Not even this was the end of the matter: independent researchers – even a handwriting expert – contradicted the imposture story and maintained that Cassidy and Phillips were one and the same.

All that can be said with certainty at the present is that Butch Cassidy and the Sundance Kid have entered the realm of American folklore, and that it now seems highly unlikely that anyone will ever be able to say with confidence where or how they died.

MATA HARI: A DOUBLE AGENT?

The question of whether or not Mata Hari was an espionage agent is debated even today, almost a century after the event. And, if she was a spy, the answer to the problem of whether she was working for the Allied side or the German side seems equally doubtful.

The First World War produced a number of intelligence agents who claimed to be the eyes of the various armies involved. Among them were Charles Lucieto, who spied for France, Miklos Soltesz (alias Nicholas

Snowden), who spied for Austria, and Marthe McKenna, who spied for Belgium. There is little or no evidence, however, that any of these secret agents made the slightest difference to the outcome of the war. Perhaps the most famous of them all was Mata Hari, who was tried and executed for her activities in 1917. Even today she remains a figure of mystery and the role she played in the war a matter of conjecture.

Mata Hari, or to give her the name by which she was baptised, Margaretha Geertruida Zelle, was born in Leeuwarden in the Netherlands in 1876, daughter of a prosperous hatter. In 1895 she married a Scottish officer, Captain Campbell MacLeod, who was in the service of the Dutch colonial army. The couple lived in Java and Sumatra until 1902 when they returned to Europe and were separated. She became an exotic dancer in Paris in 1905 and it was then that she adopted the professional name of Mata Hari, which was said to be Malay for the sun (i.e. the 'eye of the day'). Acquainted with Indian dances, attractive in appearance and apparently willing to dance virtually nude, she soon became a sensation. She took a number of lovers, some of them military officers.

Since she was the only source of much of the information relating to her espionage, the nature and extent of these activities remains cloaked in mystery to this day. According to her own account, she was recruited for espionage work by the German consul in neutral The Hague who, she said, was willing to pay her for whatever intelligence information she passed to him. After her arrest by the French she admitted doing this, but insisted that the information she had handed over was only of trivial significance and in any case was out of date when she passed it. Later she claimed to have acted for the French government in passing German military intelligence back to France from Belgium, but at the time when she began this work she neglected to tell her new masters about her earlier engagement. She did claim, however, to be on the point of enlisting the support of Ernest Augustus of Brunswick-Lüneburg for the Allied cause, by reason of his being heir to the British dukedom of Cumberland.

It was the British military authorities who first alerted the French to Mata Hari's possible duplicity, pointing out her earlier German connections. The French authorities, watching her more closely now, became increasingly doubtful of her sincerity, and in February 1917 she was arrested in Paris. It seemed at first that she had been working as a spy for both sides at the same time, and that she had, in modern parlance, been a double agent. Her activities were so complex and exaggerated that her interrogation failed to make much sense. She was imprisoned, further questioned and brought to trial before a military court in July, where she was convicted after two days and then shot by a firing squad.

Much of her trouble originated from her fertile imagination and her obsessive love of cloak-and-dagger intrigue. It now seems extremely doubtful whether any of her espionage activity was of any importance at all for either side. Nevertheless, her name became synonymous with mystery, and she entered legend as the first female spy who employed the honey trap to wheedle secrets from serving military officers.

ANNA ANDERSON – GRAND DUCHESS ANASTASIA OR CONFIDENCE TRICKSTER?

One of the great controversies of the twentieth century concerned the true fate in 1918 of the Grand Duchess Anastasia, youngest daughter of the last Tsar, Nicholas II. Was she executed along with the rest of her family in the basement of the house in Ekaterinburg where they were being detained by Bolshevik soldiers, or did she escape to tell her tale of flight and hiding in the years between the wars?

The story of the execution was related not long after the deed was committed and the account first published in Berlin early in the 1920s. On the night of 16 July 1918 the leader of the local Bolshevik Guard learned from the Central Executive Committee of the Bolshevik party that Ekaterinburg was being outflanked by White troops and by detachments of the Czech Legion (who combined to occupy the town on 26 July). He carried out a hasty execution of the tsar, his family and a number of his servants, using revolvers, bayonets and rifle butts on the victims. Anastasia was carrying the family's pet spaniel. The first hail of bullets missed her, but she fainted from the shock. When she recovered consciousness she screamed after finding her little dog dead, its head crushed by a rifle butt. She herself was then put to death by blows from bayonets and rifle butts. The bodies were wrapped in sheets and taken on a lorry to an abandoned mine nearby where they were hacked to bits with saws and axes. Efforts were made to destroy the remains using acid and by burning with petrol. They were then thrown down the mineshaft.

Legends soon spread concerning the details of these grisly murders. At least two individuals claiming to be Crown Prince Alexis turned up shortly afterwards, one in Siberia, another in Baghdad, but their impostures were flimsy and could not be sustained. The most convincing and persistent claimant to be the youngest daughter of the tsar showed up in Germany early in 1920 as a refugee from the East, spending some time in an asylum suffering from amnesia and delusions, and finally confiding her real identity as Anastasia to a nurse and a police inspector. Her story was pieced together in the form of a book, published under the title *I am Anastasia* and later turned into a film with Ingrid Bergman in the title role. She claimed to have narrowly escaped death, and to have been rescued by a Red Guard by the name of Alexander Tchaikovsky who led her to Romania from where she made her way into Germany. She made numerous attempts in the later 1920s to convince Princess Cécilie of Prussia and Anastasia's paternal aunt Grand Duchess Olga of her real identity. Olga, and more notably Grand Duke Andrew, tended to believe her at first, accepting her 'recollections' of St Petersburg and Livadiya as genuine, but this may have been wishful thinking on their part. Her identity was disputed chiefly by Anastasia's tutor who had known her since she was four and who denounced her as an impostor. She was never able to lay her hands on any of the substantial Romanov funds allegedly banked in England and in Germany on the outbreak of war. Her behaviour became increasingly erratic, and she finally returned to Germany to live the life of a recluse, going by the name of Anna Anderson.

Anna Anderson was finally categorically exposed as a fraud, but only posthumously. Bodies believed to be those of the last tsar and his family were unearthed in a shallow grave near Ekaterinburg in the mid-1990s and subjected to DNA testing in comparison with a fairly close relative of the Romanov family, Philip, the Duke of Edinburgh, husband of Queen Elizabeth II. The same tests were performed on Anna Anderson's body and they confirmed she was unconnected with the Russian royal family. Instead she was a Polish-Russian peasant by the name of Franziska Schankowska. Though the results of the first tests were not universally accepted, especially by the Russian Orthodox Church and some members of the tsar's family, the remains at Ekaterinburg were generally agreed to have been those of Nicholas II and his family, and as such were accorded solemn burial in St Petersburg in 1998.

HOWARD CARTER: DECEPTION AMONG
THE PYRAMIDS

In 1922 Howard Carter and the Earl of Carnarvon astonished the world by announcing the discovery in the Valley of the Kings of the tomb of the boy-king Tutankhamun, who was pharaoh of Egypt from about 1361 to 1352 BC. Was this discovery the stimulating and welcome surprise that it seemed, or was it instead a shabby and mercenary deception? It may now be possible to offer an explanation for what has previously been an unsolved mystery.

Howard Carter was born in 1874 in Putney, London, and was brought up in Swaffham in Norfolk. He was

the eleventh and youngest child of a rather impover-
ished middle-class father who earned his living as an
illustrator for magazines, producing delicate drawings
of birds and animals for the *Illustrated London News*.
Carter grew up with something of an inferiority
complex, uncomfortable in the presence of his betters,
resentful, and prone to furious rages if he was
wronged. Sketchily educated, he went to Thebes in
Egypt in 1891 as a draughtsman, and was employed by
Percy E. Newberry (later a professor) to ink in his
tracings of the reliefs and inscriptions on the tombs he
was working on. In 1892 he took part in Sir Flinders
Petrie's archaeological survey at el-Amarna and was
later appointed as inspector of Monuments by Gaston
Maspero, Director General of the Egyptian Service of
Antiquities, who worked for the British administration
in Egypt. He also worked for a time under Theodore
Davis, a rich American patron of Egyptology. He was,
however, dismissed from his official appointment as
the result of a quarrel with a visiting party of Frenchmen to whom he stubbornly refused to apologise. Now
he was obliged to look for another patron.

George Herbert, 5th Earl of Carnarvon and seven
years Carter's senior, had become interested in Egyptology as a result of spending a winter convalescing in
Egypt following a motor car accident in Germany in
1903. The two got on well together from the first.
Carnarvon was the sort of rich, polished and well-
connected gentleman that the altogether humbler
Carter wished he could be. They began their association in 1907 when Carter organised archaeological digs
near Luxor and later at Saqqara. Carter never recorded
why it was he set his heart on finding the tomb of
Tutankhamun, but it soon became the passion of his

life, and his work at Luxor strengthened his belief that the Valley of the Kings was a good place to begin his search.

Carter's version of what occurred was certainly an exciting story. He had been engaged in excavations in the likely area since 1907 when an underground chamber, at first believed to be the tomb, was discovered. Later another was uncovered nearby containing pottery jars filled with linen and bearing Tutankhamun's name. Though disappointed with the results, his team still continued with the work until it was interrupted by the First World War. Altogether they shifted over 200,000 tons of sand and rubble using only picks, shovels and wicker baskets. Digging resumed in 1917, but the continuing paucity of the results persuaded Carnarvon to call a halt. Only Carter's stubborn persistence at a meeting at Highclere, the earl's residence near Newbury, persuaded him to continue for a single further season – but if nothing turned up the dig was to be abandoned.

When Carter got back to Egypt in November 1922 he discovered almost immediately, but quite by chance, a step cut in the rock floor, a metre under the foundations of some workers' huts. By the next day they had uncovered twelve stone steps without reaching the foot of the stairway and the upper part of a doorway, blocked, plastered over and marked with the unbroken impressions of the ancient necropolis guards. In high excitement Carter telegraphed the good news to Carnarvon, who joined him in Egypt to open the tomb. There was evidence that the first door had been penetrated by thieves some time earlier and subsequently resealed, but a second door, about 10 metres down a sloping tunnel blocked with rubble, had not been tampered with and it was opened on 26 November, revealing animal statues, gilded chests and furniture, and masses of golden and jewelled ornaments. Carter was at first speechless, but later, waxing grandiose, he said that this was his 'day of days, the most wonderful I have ever lived through, and one whose like I can never hope to see again'.

Later efforts showed that, in addition to the ante-chamber they had first entered, there were three other chambers – an annexe, a treasury and the burial chamber itself, where there lay untouched, in the innermost of three tightly fitting coffins, the pharaoh's mummy, his head enveloped in an astonishing portrait mask of solid gold. The treasures associated with the pharaoh survived intact, along with much of his jewellery and his personal possessions. For the first time it was possible to see and understand how a pharaoh was buried. The archaeological world was bewitched by the magnitude of the find.

But was this account of the discovery of Tutan-khamen's tomb accurate, or is it an elaborate deception? According to the researcher Gerald O'Farrell, and several other leading Egyptologists, there are a number of glaring inconsistencies in Carter's story and a wealth of physical evidence to show that his account cannot be the true one.

In the first place, his picture of Egypt under the strict but benign rule of Lord Cromer before 1914 does not describe the full reality of the scene. In its lack of normal, civilised rules and its ruthlessness, the atmosphere of pre-war Cairo was a curious mixture of the competitive strife of the Californian gold-rush and the scandalous intrigue associated with the Orient. There was a lively antiquities market where museums and private collectors jostled for prizes. Against this background, Carter worked almost single-handedly in the Valley of the Kings at cataloguing and reproducing the many tomb paintings there. He learned hieroglyphics the better to understand the inscriptions, and fluent Arabic the better to get on with the locals. Some of his associates went so far as to suggest that Carter had 'gone native'. In particular he made the acquaintance of two locals, Makarios and Andraos, who convinced him they knew of unopened tombs. Carter struck a secret deal with them whereby they split the proceeds of their pilfering fifty-fifty. He also made the acquaintance of the el-Rassul family of tomb-robbers who operated from Querna next to the Valley of the Kings. His Arab accomplices showed him an impressive sixteen-column hall alongside an earlier tomb (possibly that of Tutankhamun's father), which was so lavish that he could only suppose it led to a further as yet undiscovered tomb.

Although he found out that many of the tombs in the area were connected by a network of underground passages, Carter was unable to make much further progress at the time. One of his difficulties arose from sheer lack of money. Soon, however, he gained cash from his association with the affluent dilettante Theodore Davis, with whom he made a bargain. Davis held a concession allowing him to dig in the Valley of the Kings until 1914, and in return for working his concession Carter, as Inspector of Monuments, arranged to let Davis retain any duplicate antiquities that were found. After his dismissal from his official post, Carter, for a time desperately short of money, struck up a much more fruitful (though less legal) relationship with Carnarvon in 1907. Over the next few years, these two dug up and smuggled out of Egypt a mass of valuable artefacts, some of which went into Carnarvon's private collection, others being sold on the commercial market to collectors or to institutions such as the Metropolitan Museum of New York. Carter even kept some of the finds himself.

The discoveries which Carter's 'diaries' dated to after the First World War had in reality been made long before the conflict started. The steps leading down to an unopened tomb had actually been discovered in 1907, though the tomb itself was not found until 1913 when Carter entered it from the maze of interconnecting passages and through the back wall. While Davis was still excavating above, Carter was engaged 2 metres below in shifting many of the gold items he found and spiriting them away. He feared that Davis was suspicious of his activities and was on tenterhooks that the other man would break through from above and find him at work. However, he was able to distract Davis's attention and stop the approach of his workers, telling them that the dig had to be stopped because the roadway was in danger of collapse. When Davis's concession expired he breathed more freely (Davis then left Egypt and shortly afterwards died). But by this time Carter's programme of grave-robbing was in full swing and continued throughout the First World War.

Perhaps the most important reason why Carter was obliged to falsify the events leading to the supposed discovery in 1922 was a political one. Having annexed Egypt during the war, Britain gave the country back its independence in 1922. Its new government promptly became much more alert to the need to preserve its own heritage and antiquities, and threatened an investigation of recent archaeological activities – if only to claim a share in their marketing. Carter was thoroughly alarmed, not least because his own activities as an official had been so reprehensible. He hastily conferred with his patron. The two of them brazenly decided on a bluff, covering their recent criminal acts with the pretence that they had only just discovered the tomb. So in the summer of 1922 Carter built a wall where he had broken through into the rear of the tomb, plastering it in a lifelike fashion and even decorating it with appropriate paintings; then he tunnelled up to the valley floor to make an exit (presently used as the entrance), sealed it with a stone door and attached fake seals. He even went to the lengths of filling in the exit tunnel with rubble in the interests of authenticity. Finally he faked the whole of his working diary to document the steps leading to the 'discovery'. The seals would be discovered as fakes, whereupon Carter could claim that the tomb had been raided in antiquity. Under the newly introduced regulations the Egyptian government could claim only half the value of the heavier items that remained (after Carter had already creamed off 80 per cent of the smaller valuables), and in the light of Carter's 'diary' entries, it would be unable to claim the entire find, which it could have done if the discovery were completely new.

Unfortunately Carter made a number of fairly elementary blunders. For one thing, though he was a very competent artist, he could not entirely capture the style of Egyptian tomb paintings, and the figures he painted on his newly plastered wall were drawn not quite in proportion. Furthermore, some of the exquisitely constructed woodwork with which the tomb was furnished was found to be bruised by marks from heavy hammers as if it had been cobbled together in a hurry by amateurs. But most seriously of all, his exit tunnel, which he maintained was the main entrance, was less than 2 metres wide, while the axle-shafts on the chariots that the tomb contained were about 2½ metres. How were those responsible for the funeral supposed to have got them down there? Carter was obliged to saw through the axles and dismantle the chariots – an act of quite breath-taking vandalism. The excuse he offered was that the tomb architects had been careless in their planning and the tomb workers clumsy in their efforts – though carelessness and clumsiness were scarcely what would have been expected of workers engaged in anything so solemn as burying a king-emperor who was also a god.

Nevertheless Carter and his felonious patron got away with their bold deception. The tomb made world headlines. On his return to London after a splendid reception arranged to celebrate its opening, Carnarvon was lionised by scientific experts everywhere and even had an audience at Buckingham Palace with George V. To avoid the close attentions of the press, and also further to enhance his profits from the scam, he negotiated an extremely profitable deal with *The Times* (an initial fee of £5,000 and 75 per cent royalties on subsequent stories) giving it exclusive rights to report on his archaeological work. Carnarvon was even contemplating a deal with MGM for a film on the subject of his discovery of the tomb.

Unfortunately, less than a year later he died suddenly, reputedly as the result of an infected mosquito bite. The press seized on the tragedy and made a splash by inventing the story of the 'mummy's curse' – a legend reinforced by the subsequent deaths of a number of others of the party who had made the first entry into the burial chamber. Carter at first pooh-poohed the idea (he is supposed to have said to anyone who referred to the question: 'The answer is spherical and in the plural') but he later encouraged it. It served as a blind to distract attention from the more dubious aspects of the supposed discovery – in particular why the pharaoh had been buried in such an inconveniently small tomb, and how those who had arranged his funeral had managed to cram such a wealth of treasures into four such tiny rooms, none of which was bigger than 6 metres by 4. Meantime, Carter restricted public access to the tomb on the pretext of preserving the integrity of his find, and locked up a nearby empty tomb which he used as his workshop to keep it from prying eyes.

The Egyptians, however, regarded the whole affair with deep suspicion. Zaghlul Pasha, leader of the Egyptian Wafd party and head of the government under King Fuad, disputed Carter's claim even to a half-share of the findings. He suggested that Carnarvon's licence to dig expressly excluded his rights over anything that he found – a claim that neither Carter nor Carnarvon disputed since both pretended that the whole expedition was purely in the interests of science and neither wished to be made to appear as mercenary as he really was. Government officials chafed at their exclusion from the site and later forced an entry to the tomb on the pretext of taking an inventory of its contents, four-fifths of which had already been stolen. They also broke into Carter's workshop where they found a wooden crate labelled 'Red Wine'. It contained a decorative head of

Tutankhamun rising from a lotus blossom fashioned from wood. They were furious at the theft, rightly suspecting there had been many others. As a result they suspended all archaeological digs in the country, denying to foreign antiquarians the right to excavate except under the closest scrutiny. Carter, retired from his life's work, continued to lodge at the Windsor Palace Hotel, Luxor, almost within sight of the Valley of the Kings, but living now in idleness. He had, however, done his merchandising well and was now a rich man.

The Egyptian government was quite right. After Carnarvon's death his widow, Lady Evelyn Herbert, sold the bulk of her husband's collection to the Metropolitan Museum in New York for the then enormous sum of £40,000. The chairman of the board of the museum confessed to having been given a ring by Carnarvon in 1921 which bore the cartouche of Tutankhamun, a ring that had been in circulation seven years before the tomb had been 'discovered'. Later hundreds of items identified as coming from Tutankhamun's tomb were found scattered among the leading museums of Europe and America. The sheer mass of Tutankhamun treasures displayed in museums and private collections throughout the world was so great that it was a physical impossibility that they could ever have been packed into the four small chambers that Carter pretended were the whole tomb. As Gerald O'Farrell put it, the result was 'like trying to convince us that all the contents of Buckingham Palace had been discovered in Anne Hathaway's cottage'.

When Carter died in England in 1939 he bequeathed the bulk of his estate to his niece, Phyllis Walker, and it was found to contain many precious objects, including a delicately shaped and enamelled perfume bottle from the tomb. All of these had been stolen. She later returned these objects to Egypt through the hands of Fuad's successor, King Farouk.

The mystery of Carnarvon and Carter thus remains officially unsolved, though archaeologists may make an educated guess as to the truth about their activities. On balance it seems likely that they were not two great scientists, fortunate to make one of the most significant archaeological finds of all time in the Valley of the Kings, but were rather, among a host of others, a successful but otherwise rather ordinary pair of grave-robbers.

MALLORY AND IRVINE: DID THEY CLIMB EVEREST?

In 1953, the year of the coronation of Elizabeth II, international recognition heralded the feat of Sir Edmund Hillary and Sherpa Tenzing Norgay in conquering Mount Everest in Tibet, at over 29,000 feet the highest mountain peak in the world. But in 1999 a joint Anglo–US climbing expedition discovered the mummified remains of a previous climber close to the summit. This posed the question of whether in fact the mountain had already been successfully climbed in an earlier expedition by Mallory and Irvine, before Queen Elizabeth had even been born.

In June 1924 George Leigh Mallory, an experienced and resourceful climber, made an attempt to conquer Everest in the company of a younger companion,

Andrew ('Sandy') Irvine, a 22-year-old mountaineer of much less experience but skilful at handling the oxygen supplies with which the expedition was for the first time equipped.

Mallory, born in 1886 and hence at the time of the expedition already thirty-eight years old, was a happily married Englishman who had tried to conquer Everest on two previous occasions. He had made a reconnoitring expedition with a party in 1921, and they had become the first to be acquainted with a Buddhist monastery at 23,500 feet, within sight of the summit, which acted as the base for later attempts and which is still visited today by climbing parties approaching Everest. The 1921 expedition had, however, been a failure and Mallory had returned home determined to try again.

He made a second attempt in 1923. In 1924 he was making his third and, in view of his age, probably final effort. The climbing party set off from Base Camp, from there making their long upwards slog the length of an approach glacier to Camp 2, then to Advanced Base Camp 3 at 25,000 feet and to Camp 4 at the foot of the North Face of the mountain, and finally the much shorter distances through Camp 5 to Camp 6 at 27,000 feet, both camps situated on the lower slopes of the North Face itself. Here on 6 June the two climbers made their final preparations for their attempt on the summit with their camera and other equipment. On the morning of 8 June one of the party who was lower down saw Mallory and Irvine going strongly towards the summit before the weather closed in. The climb, along the ridge of the Col, is a distance of more than a mile and made difficult by the exposed position, the great altitude and the oxygen tanks that the two were carrying. The final difficulty was the three 'steps' – three discontinuities in the terrain of the ridge – of which the most serious was the second. The two were approaching this when they were last spotted. They were never seen again.

The loss of Mallory and Irvine took some time to be reported back to Britain, where it eventually appeared in all the newspapers. Another expedition in 1933 found Irvine's ice-axe at about the position where the pair had last been seen, but the two men were never found. It was only in 1976 that a climber, a member of a Chinese and Japanese party attempting Everest, reported finding the corpse of a previous European fatality at 8,150 metres (26,755 feet), and in much the sort of location that indicated it could be either Mallory or Irvine. The climber said he had found the body only about ten minutes away from the place where he had camped, but since there was no precise record of where this was, his report was not of much help.

Thus it was that in May 1999 a fresh expedition made a determined effort to locate the body. After a protracted search of the slopes on the North Col the semi-mummified remains of the earlier climber were discovered. The body was on a ledge and was that of Mallory. The disposition of the remains suggested that he had fallen several hundred feet and had broken his leg in the fall. The hands were still clawed from scrabbling at the rock face where, according to the recommended technique, he had been trying to arrest his slide. He was still wearing his hobnail boots and six or seven layers of clothing, now compacted together and tissue-paper thin. Inside his shirt collar was a label bearing the name of 'Mallory'. However, most of his back was bare where the clothes had been pulled from it. There were still ropes secured around the body. The party viewed the body, and then, with some misgivings, searched it. They found personal letters that were still legible, and even an unpaid bill for some items of equipment. They found his climbing goggles in his pocket, and an altimeter, but this was broken. There was no camera. After brief prayers the 1999 party buried Mallory's body by piling over it a cairn of stones in the hope it would never be disturbed again.

Many of the 1999 climbers were of the opinion that Mallory had in fact conquered Everest. They thought that the final stages to the summit were laborious but not impossible. They believed that he knew that this was probably his last attempt on the mountain, and that he was determined to succeed, even if it killed him. They believed he could well have overcome the difficulties of the second and third 'steps' and reached the summit during that fateful day of 8 June. Though they never found his camera, they believed that the fact they found his goggles in his pocket strongly suggested that the light was fading and that he was on his way down from the summit when the accident happened. They even thought they saw Mallory's personal determination to conquer Everest still stamped on his corpse seventy-five years after the event.

Nevertheless the mystery of whether Mallory and Irvine succeeded in climbing Everest remains unsolved. The find of a camera would have provided irrefutable evidence of success, but, even without it, those who found Mallory's body still believe that there was a better than evens chance he scaled the summit nearly thirty years before Hillary.

WHO BURNED THE REICHSTAG?

*The burning of the German Reichstag early in 1933
created a mystery that took years to resolve.
Clouds of left- and right-wing rhetoric have long
obscured the truth. Even today the responsibility
for the outrage is sometimes debated.*

On the evening of 27 February 1933 the German
Reichstag building went up in flames. Hitler, who had
been appointed German Chancellor only a month
earlier but who lacked a parliamentary majority and
was badly in need of an anti-Red scare, decided to
make what profit he could from the event. He had
already denounced the Communists for subversion,
but lacked convincing evidence for his charge. This act
of arson provided him with an excellent opportunity
to smear his opponents.

The Nazis said the outrage was the work of the
Communists, and afterwards staged a trial of the
alleged incendiaries before the High Court in Leipzig.
However, the trial – in spite of the best efforts of the
chief prosecutor, Goering – was a failure, chiefly
because of the brilliant advocacy of the accused. At the
same time the obvious eagerness of the Nazis to secure
a conviction led naturally to the belief that they were
themselves responsible for the outrage. A number of
leading historians, including Alan Bullock, repeat this
erroneous idea. What really happened?

At about nine o'clock that evening a university
student who had been studying in the library was on
his way home when he heard the noise of breaking
glass and thought he saw a shadowy figure climbing
into the Reichstag building through a first-floor

window. He fetched a policeman, but they could not find anyone. The policeman did, however, discover flames and at 9.15 called the fire brigade. At first they could not gain access. When they did, they wasted time on small fires in the corridor. It was 9.40 before the brigade's full strength was mustered and sixty appliances were sent to the building. By that time, it was well alight, and soon it was irretrievably lost. A minor Nazi figure, knowing that Goering, who was President of the Reichstag, Hitler and Goebbels were at a party nearby, telephoned them with the news. At first they simply did not believe it. Hitler, however, sensing a chance to turn the situation to his advantage, worked himself up into a rage and demanded that Communists be rounded up and shot, since this was clearly a Communist plot.

Meantime, a half-naked young Dutchman by the name of Marinus van der Lubbe had been arrested in the building and taken to the nearest police station. He was then questioned until the early hours, and gave a full account of his behaviour. His motives were unclear, based, it appeared, on some vague resentment, but it seemed that he thought the burning of the building would act as a 'beacon for revolt'. He impressed his interrogators with his clarity and intelligence. He described where he had bought petrol and firelighters, and told his listeners how he had stripped off his clothes before soaking them in the fuel, scattering them about and setting light to them. The police checked the details and established that they were all true. Fire officials confirmed that the arson was technically possible, given the design of the building and the fact that its central dome created a chimney effect. This, together with the regular oiling of its panelling for cleaning purposes, made it an ideal site for such a crime. They eventually agreed that van der Lubbe had conceived and committed the act alone, and that the Communist party was not involved.

This explanation was quite unacceptable to Hitler and his associates. At the ensuing trial they ignored the evidence of the investigators and their evaluation of van der Lubbe's personality, insisting on making him out to be the half-witted dupe of the Communist party, put up to the job by his unscrupulous masters. They accused him of being an active Communist, though in fact he had only vaguely socialistic left-wing views and was unknown to the Communists. They stressed the improbability of one man starting such a massive conflagration unaided and called numerous technical experts to prove that he could not have done it without assistance. However, many of these experts were not fire officers or policemen but professors of chemistry and criminology, some of whom had never even visited the Reichstag before. Furthermore, only one of the accused – Torgler, leader of the Communist group in parliament – had been anywhere near the Reichstag that evening, and he had left at 8 p.m. The others, the leading Bulgarian Communist Dimitrov and two other Bulgarians, had been nowhere near, and in any case had no connection with, nor had even heard of, van der Lubbe.

This was awkward for the High Court judges. Before convicting, they would usually have preferred to have had some evidence of the guilt of the accused. Van der Lubbe made no bones over his guilt. He spoke clearly, coherently and accurately. He tried for six hours to convince the court that no one had instigated his behaviour, and rejected the evidence of Hitler's experts, saying: 'I was there, and they were not. I know it can be done because I did it.' Most impressive was the court performance of Georgi Dimitrov, the leading Communist on trial. He was lucid, convincing, and ran rings round the chief prosecutor, Goering, whom he reduced to gibbering incoherence.

In the end the High Court found van der Lubbe guilty, and, even though arson was not a capital crime until Hitler made it so retrospectively, sentenced him to death. He was duly executed by beheading with an axe. The four Communists were acquitted, but the court added the rider that van der Lubbe must have had assistance from 'persons unknown'.

Dimitrov put his finger on the weakness of the Nazis' case in court when he accused Goering to his face: 'Van der Lubbe had help. He did not get it from me. Therefore he must have got it from you.' The Communists – who staged a counter-trial in London at which they proved to their own satisfaction that it was the Nazis who were responsible for the outrage – made much play with a 'secret' passage said to carry phone and electric cables and central heating pipes to Goering's house nearby (where the original informant who telephoned Goering at his party lodged) and alleged that the Brownshirts had used this to penetrate the building. There they laid the fires themselves, and at the last minute pushed van der Lubbe through the window to be picked up by the police and take the rap. This story was equally unlikely, and in any case ignored the fact that at 8.45 the building had been visited by a postman delivering the deputies' mail who neither saw, smelt nor heard anything suspicious. The evidence of this humble postman, who was not even called at the trial, shows that the Reichstag building was empty when van der Lubbe broke in at nine o'clock.

The most likely explanation for the blaze therefore appears to be that neither the Communists nor the Nazis were responsible. Van der Lubbe did it all by himself.

WHO WAS MR GORSKY? NEIL ARMSTRONG'S PECULIAR GREETING FROM THE MOON

One of the oddest mysteries of the space age began on 20 July 1969 at the time of the US moon landing. It was on this occasion that Neil Armstrong, commander of the Apollo lunar module, first set foot on the surface of the Moon. His first words were televised to Earth and were heard by millions: 'That's one small step for Man; one giant leap for Mankind.'

A few moments later, just before he re-entered the lander, it was said that he muttered the enigmatic remark 'Good luck, Mr Gorsky.' His companions aboard the mission were puzzled, since they were unfamiliar with the name. Back at NASA headquarters in Houston some of those who claimed also to have heard it thought this was the name of someone Armstrong had encountered during the long weeks of his training for the mission, or of a rival Soviet cosmonaut. However, on checking – and there was no doubt in their minds that they had heard it – they could find no Gorsky in either the Soviet or the American space programmes.

Over the years many people questioned Armstrong as to what exactly the words 'Good luck, Mr Gorsky' meant, but he always just smiled.* He never offered any word of explanation for his actions until 5 July 1995 in Tampa Bay, Florida. Then, following a speech, a news reporter brought up the 26-year-old question. This time it is said that Armstrong finally responded. He told his audience that Mr Gorsky had now died so he felt free to answer the question.

In 1938, when he was a kid in a small Mid-West town, Armstrong was playing ball with a friend in his backyard. His friend hit the ball, which landed in his neighbour's yard. The ball fell close to the bedroom windows of the single-storey house owned by an elderly Jewish couple, a Mr and Mrs Gorsky. The young Armstrong climbed over the fence and went to pick up the ball. As he did so, he heard Mrs Gorsky indoors yelling at Mr Gorsky: 'Sex! You say you want sex! You'll get sex when the kid next door walks on the Moon!'

* The veracity of the story seems still to be a matter of heated debate. For every person who affirms it as the truth there seems to be another who says it is all a joke, and that the reason why Armstrong refused to answer his questioners was that for him the joke had worn rather thin.

3

Murder and Mayhem

WAS THERE A BLACK HOLE OF CALCUTTA?

After it was granted its royal charter in 1600 the English East India Company traded with the Indian subcontinent, tried to avoid becoming involved in internal Indian politics, and made fortunes for its principal employees. But it could not keep out of politics altogether, and used native troops under a handful of company-trained officers to protect its trade and personnel. The English government avoided involvement except in the event of war, unlike the French government which supported its East India Company to the hilt and encouraged it to challenge the English company in the latter's traditional strongholds. As a result, England's political involvement in India became necessary if the English company was to survive. One event was crucial in converting influential English opinion to an interventionist policy – the infamous Black Hole of Calcutta on 21 June 1756. On that night 123 English prisoners were said to have suffocated on the orders of Siraj-ud-Daula, nawab (ruler) of Bengal. Thenceforth England regarded all Indian rulers as savages like Siraj and considered that they were unfit to govern. From this it was but a short step to the establishment of partial and eventually complete English political control over the areas in which the East

*India Company traded. But what is the truth of the
Black Hole? Did 123 die? Did Siraj-ud-Daula
deliberately order their deaths? Indeed, did the
Black Hole really happen at all?*

Although England and France had earlier agreed not
to encroach on each other's trade and spheres of
influence in India, England was alarmed in the 1750s
to see the French taking control of Hyderabad
and parts of the Deccan. Early in 1756 the French
seized four East India Company depots in the Deccan.
To the north, Siraj-ud-Daula viewed these developments with some alarm. He had only recently become
the nawab of Bengal and unless he could curb
European encroachments he seemed unlikely to
remain ruler for long. He therefore decided to throw
in his lot with the French, hoping he could play them
off against the English and retain his independence in
so doing.

The Seven Years' War began in May 1756, although
hostilities in the West Indies, Canada and the Mediterranean had been in progress for some months. Siraj-
ud-Daula may not yet have heard of the declaration
but he would have known of the virtual state of war
between France and England. He therefore captured
the trading depot at Kasimbazar and proceeded to
attack Calcutta and the East India Company's base at
Fort William with an army of over 30,000 men. Its
defenders were 230 Europeans. The governor decided
that the fort was undefendable against such overwhelming odds and escaped downriver with the
European women and children, abandoning most of
the garrison to its fate. It put up what resistance it
could, but was soon forced into inevitable surrender.

What happened next was to pass into Indian folk-lore. News reached England that after the garrison's surrender 146 Europeans had to be accommodated. It was the night of 21 June. The hottest month in India precedes the monsoon, and the monsoon did not normally reach Bengal in full intensity until July. In June, therefore, night temperatures usually remain stiflingly high. This was such a night. Yet on Suraj-ud-Daula's specific orders the 146 men were conducted to an airless room measuring less than 8 by 6 metres, and they were confined without water. He ordered that he was not to be disturbed. So the pathetic cries of the room's inmates for water and for mercy went unheeded: the guard had been given instructions neither to give succour to the prisoners nor to disturb the nawab until morning. It was said that men stood on each other, gasping for air; that those who could placed their faces next to the cell grille or next to the tiny window. Although the prisoners were dying one by one the cruel guards stood by and offered no relief. By next morning only 23 survived and 123 lay dead in the cell.

This account was substantiated by one of the survivors, John Zephaniah Holwell, who published the sole contemporary account on his return to England. It was not contradicted by other survivors, except on small details such as the size of the room and whether or not it contained a window. It made a powerful and horrifying tale, and substantial royalties for its author. Nor could Siraj-ud-Daula offer any refutation since he was murdered in the custody of his treacherous successor, Mir Jaffer, in the following year, soon after his own defeat by Robert Clive at the battle of Plassey. It would be gratifying to think that his assassins were motivated by the horror of the Black Hole, but it is much more likely that they were emboldened by the victory at Plassey and suborned by the East India Company's money.

Holwell's account remained virtually unchallenged, although it was accepted that some of its detail may have been amplified for publication. Not until the early twentieth century did anyone question the substance of the narrative. Subsequent challenges varied in degree from those who queried Holwell's minutiae to those who doubted whether any Black Hole took place at all. The differences between Holwell and his fellow survivors made a good starting point. If the room was only 8 metres by 6 metres, then each of the prisoners would have had barely a third of a square metre of space to stand, sit or lie in. It would have been virtually impossible, even at bayonet point, for the whole 146 to have squeezed into such a space. Those accounts suggesting an even smaller space must be mistaken about the number of prisoners. And to contain 146 the room would need to have been not just larger, but much larger. No satisfactory identification of the cell was made in the years immediately following the Black Hole, so its size and whether or not it contained a grille or a window could never be established. If it was a large storeroom, it might well have been windowless; if it was a prison cell, it would probably have had both grille and window, but it would have been much smaller than 8 by 6 metres. Neither the nawab nor the company would have had need for extensive prison accommodation.

The suffocating conditions have been queried too. Statements that the temperature on a June night in Calcutta does not fall below 32°C (90°F) are belied by the meteorological statistics: the average daily minimum in June and July is 26°C (79°F), but with the humidity accompanying the start of the monsoon, conditions in an overcrowded room would still have been intolerable.

Those who doubted the Black Hole story altogether have been undermined by the findings of Indian historians. They conclude that the Black Hole definitely took place, but have found that only 43 of the original garrison of Fort William could not be accounted for, so at most 43 died. Since there were 23 known survivors, this makes a maximum number imprisoned in the Black Hole of 66. They also argue that it is unlikely that Siraj-ud-Daula would have been directly concerned in the fate of the prisoners; in playing off the British against the French, an act of such gross cruelty would surely have been counter-productive. It is more likely that after a strenuous day Siraj retired to his quarters, leaving a subordinate officer to put the captives in a temporary cell where they were unintentionally left overnight. If so, stories of piteous pleadings with the guards can be discounted since if the prisoners were left unintentionally, there would have been no guards to hear their pleas and certainly no instructions not to provide them with water. Even with these modifications it is still a gruesome story. Two-thirds of the prisoners died in what was more likely a terrible accident than deliberate murder. The full truth will never be known, but the popular account is certainly a misconception.

Holwell's story, therefore, needs considerable qualification. He turned a tragedy into a great drama in which he posed as the hero, and, indeed, he was later rewarded with the governorship of Bengal. Clive used the incident to intrigue with Mir Jaffer, Siraj's right-hand man, and to justify his destruction of Siraj's army at the battle of Plassey in 1757. To Englishmen the Black Hole made India synonymous with treachery and barbarism and confirmed that the Indians were unfit to govern themselves. When Clive and later Warren Hastings resorted to questionable methods in their government of Bengal they could point to the Black Hole as far worse than anything they had done. So while the exact circumstances of the Black Hole still remain something of a mystery, there is no question about its importance in determining the course of Indian history.

WHO WAS SWEET FANNY ADAMS?

The expression 'sweet Fanny Adams' came to be used as naval slang in the middle years of the nineteenth century to describe the stew (usually made with mutton) supplied to the sailors in their mess by the ship's cooks. By extension this meaning was widened to cover other items of the sailors' fare until it came in the end to mean to servicemen anything that was unappetising, or of little or no value. In more modern times the initials in the abbreviation 'sweet FA' have come to acquire a grosser sexual significance as 'sweet fuck-all'.

The original Frances (or Fanny) Adams was a little girl from Alton in Hampshire. At the age of eight she was murdered in the hop fields at Flood Meadows, Alton, while helping to gather in the harvest. She went missing on 24 August 1867 and her body was later found where it had been left by her assailant. She was suspected of having been sexually assaulted before she was killed, but this was never finally established since the body had been mutilated and dismembered into at least twenty fragments by the killer. Later in the year a certain Frederick Baker was tried and convicted for the murder, and in one of the last public executions in Britain he was hanged at Winchester on Christmas Eve 1867.

The maritime connection with this macabre little story is not immediately obvious, but probably relates to the introduction at about the same time of canned meat into the rations provided for the Royal Navy. The sailors did not care for the new meat and made the joke that the cans must have contained the last remains of the unfortunate Fanny. This story has some loose resemblance to the prejudice against the cans of corned beef from the stockyards of Chicago later in the century, when it was commonly asserted that one or more workmen in the canning plant had fallen into the machinery which had not been stopped, so that their remains contaminated the much boasted purity of the product.

The truth is that the remains of Frances Adams lie interred in Alton cemetery, close to St Lawrence's church, where the girl's grave is still clearly marked and well maintained.

WHO WAS JACK THE RIPPER?

In 1888, the East End of London became the scene of a series of ghastly murders popularly attributed to the figure known to history as 'Jack the Ripper'.

From that day to this the cases remain unsolved. Many suggestions have been made about the villain's identity, some of them extremely fanciful, and questions have been asked as to why this series of murders has never been solved. While it remains unlikely that the former mystery will ever be cracked, it is perhaps possible to suggest reasons for the latter.

The killings, nine in number between 1888 and 1889 with a tenth in 1891, became known as the White-chapel murders, since most of them took place in or near the tangle of dim, narrow streets and courtyards of that portion of the East End of London. The victims were working-class women, some of them prostitutes, given to heavy drinking and late nights, as well as, by trade, to the company of men of various classes. Of this string of murders, five were similar in method and apparent motive, and were probably committed by the same hand. However, it seems likely that not all ten crimes were the work of one killer. Some may have been copycat murders; others may not have been part of the series at all but merely mistakenly identified as such in the alarmist atmosphere then prevailing. There is, indeed, no definitive proof that Jack the Ripper ever existed – he may have been the product of the hysterical press speculation of the time. Indeed the blood-curdling 'Dear Boss' letter – written in red ink to Tom Bullen of the Central News Agency, Ludgate Circus, for forwarding to Chief Constable Williamson of Scotland Yard – may itself have been a hoax. In it the author enthusiastically adopted for himself the popular nickname of the 'Ripper' given him by the public and gloated over the gruesome details of the crimes.

In the course of the investigation, about 100 people were arrested and interviewed in connection with the murders, and a further, quite different, three principal suspects were named in a report made by Assistant Chief Constable M.L. Macnaghten in 1894, but no charge was ever brought before a court in any of the cases. Accusing fingers were even pointed at the Duke of Clarence, eldest son of the future Edward VII, and a recent film has suggested that Queen Victoria herself colluded in the suppression of the case against him; but this suspicion is extremely fanciful and must remain in the realm of fiction. Another recent suggestion has come from an American crime-writer, Patricia Cornwell, who has come to the apparently surprising conclusion that the evidence points to the murderer being the painter Walter Sickert.

The first Whitechapel murder was that of 45-year-old Emma Elizabeth Smith, lodging in Spitalfields, who was assaulted and robbed by three men, one of them a youth of about nineteen, on the evening of 2 April 1888. She had been drinking and was on her way home. The attackers beat her about the head and chest, tore her ear and thrust a broom handle or similar blunt instrument 'up her passage' (i.e. her vagina) with great violence, as the result of which her peritoneum was ruptured. She was taken to hospital where she died of peritonitis the following day. This assault, culminating though it did in murder, was committed by a gang in the furtherance of robbery and did not have the typical sexual overtones of a Ripper killing.

The second murder was that of Martha Tabram, also known as Turner, during the early hours of 10 August 1888. She was a prostitute, aged thirty-seven and living in rooms at George Yard, Whitechapel. She had been drinking the previous evening in the company of another prostitute known as Pearly Poll and two soldiers, but her murder appeared to have taken place some time after that. The two soldiers, a corporal and a private in the Guards, were later identified, interviewed and exonerated of the crime. The victim's clothing was disarranged, and she had been stabbed with great violence thirty-nine times with some kind of dagger in various parts of her body. The blow to the heart alone was sufficient to cause death, but the knife attack was obviously a frenzied one and had continued for some time. The attack suggested that her assailant was motivated by an overwhelming hatred of prostitutes, though there was no evidence of sexual interference either before or after death.

The third murder took place on 31 August 1888. It was that of Mary Ann Nichols, forty-five years old and another prostitute, who had drifted from lodging to lodging but at the time of her death was staying at Flower and Dean Street, Spitalfields. She was found in the early hours of that morning with her clothes thrust up above the knees. Her clothing was cut, torn and badly bloodstained, but had not been removed. Her throat had been cut from left to right and her windpipe severed, her abdomen slashed upwards in a jagged cut from the pelvis to the ribcage, her stomach punctured, and she had a number of minor stabs to her private parts, all made with a stout, narrow-bladed weapon. The idea previously entertained that the assailant was left-handed seemed to be confirmed by the configuration of the wounds. For the first time suspicion was cast on one John Pizer (also known as 'Leather Apron'), who was known to have ill-used and sometimes blackmailed prostitutes, but when he was detained and questioned it proved impossible to proceed against him. The murder, nonetheless, did seem to conform closely to the killings associated with the Ripper.

The fourth murder was that of Annie Chapman in the early hours of 8 September 1888 in the backyard of the house where she was lodging in Hanbury Street, Spitalfields. She was also a prostitute and was forty-five years old. Her throat had been cut so deeply that her head was almost severed from her body. She had been partially disembowelled, her small intestines arranged about her body, and her stomach and larger intestines exposed by two flaps of flesh roughly cut from her torso. Her womb, bladder and the upper part of her vagina had been cut out altogether and removed. The murder had been effected violently but with considerable surgical skill. The weapon was said to have been a small amputating knife or a well-ground slaughterman's knife, narrow and thin. Once again the crime conformed to the pattern associated with the Ripper. Suspicion was this time cast on Joseph (or Jacob) Isenschmidt, a former butcher, said to be insane, who allegedly was in the habit of carrying large butcher's knives about with him. Also questioned in connection with the crime were men by the names of Edward McKenna, John Pizer (again) and Edward Stanley. But no case could be brought against any of them. For the first time, questions were raised by the public and in the press about police competence.

The fifth murder took place shortly before 1 a.m. on Sunday 30 September 1888 inside the gates of Duffield's Yard, Berner Street, Commercial Road East. The victim was Elizabeth Stride (known as Long Liz although she was only 5 feet 2 inches), a Swedish immigrant who had had the maiden name of Gustafsdotter. She was a local prostitute. Her body was lying on its side, knees drawn up, but her clothing was not disarranged. A small bunch of flowers was still pinned to her dress, and she was holding a packet of cachous in her hand. Her throat had been deeply gashed from the left, the carotid artery severed, death resulting from the loss of several pints of blood. She had not been robbed but still had several small possessions about her and sixpence in the pocket of her underskirt. There were no other injuries and no evidence of sexual motives for the killing.

That same night Catherine Eddowes, a hawker by trade, forty-three years old and often given to strong drink, was released from Bishopsgate Street police station and made her way eastwards to Mitre Square, Aldgate, in the City of London, where she became the victim of the sixth murder. The killing took place less than 3 miles from, and only three-quarters of a hour after, the murder of Elizabeth Stride. Eddowes was found sprawled on the ground, her throat cut; the cause of death was the severing of the left carotid artery. Her mutilations were inflicted posthumously. Her face was badly disfigured by a sharp instrument such as a surgeon's knife, her nose cut off, her eyelids slit, her vocal cords cut through. Then her body was systematically disembowelled: her abdomen exposed by tearing open her clothes, her intestines drawn out and draped over her right shoulder, a piece of the intestines detached from her body and placed alongside it, her liver stabbed and then carved open, her uterus cut through, and her left kidney cut out and removed. There was remarkably little blood on her clothing, and her assailant had shown considerable speed and anatomical skill in his proceedings. Half the stolen kidney was later posted to the president of the Whitechapel Vigilance Committee with a little note saying: 'T'other piece I fried and ate it was very nice'; he handed it over at once to the City Police.

There were two other bizarre features of this murder: nearby was found a bloodstained apron (which renewed earlier fears of attacks by 'Leather Apron' though in fact it was made of white calico), and chalked on the wall over the discarded garment was the slogan 'The Juwes are the men who will not be blamed for nothing'. The locality, then as now, was inhabited by Jews of all nationalities, a number of whom had already been questioned, though the police had sought in vain to interview one Lipski in connection with this and earlier crimes – indeed there was some doubt whether in fact he existed, or whether this was a slang term applied to all Jews. The episode showed, however, the prevalence of anti-Semitic feeling at the time and throughout the case it continued to lurk below the surface.

The seventh murder (the last of the Whitechapel crimes now known as the canonical five Ripper killings, the others being of Nichols, Chapman, Stride and Eddowes), followed on 9 November 1888. The victim was Mary Jane Kelly, twenty-four years old and a prostitute, living in a single ground-floor room in a three-storey house at 26 Dorset Street, Spitalfields. Her mutilations were the most grotesque of all. Her throat and larynx had been cut, her face gashed in all directions and her nose, cheeks, eyebrows and ears completely or partly removed. She was lying flat on her back and naked, her legs wide apart, and the entire surface of her abdomen and thighs had been cut away.

Her breasts had been cut off, the abdominal cavity emptied of its viscera and her uterus, kidneys, liver, spleen and intestines arranged about the room. The pericardium had been opened and her heart removed. The public outcry was immediate and hysterical. No one knew whether the treatment meted out to the corpse was part of some cabbalistic ritual or whether it signified nothing more than the loathing and sadistic contempt felt by the murderer for his victim. Whichever it was, the East End was petrified. The chief constable of the Metropolitan Police was hounded into resignation; even the queen was disturbed by the case and posed a number of pertinent questions about the police investigations. This reassured the public somewhat, though it did nothing to scotch rumours that no less a person than Lord Salisbury had discouraged further investigation because the Ripper was actually a member of the House of Lords.

Shortly afterwards, on 22 November 1888, Annie Farmer, of Featherstone Street, City Road, a woman of forty, separated from her husband by reason of her dissolute habits, reported being picked up by a companion who had treated her to a number of drinks. When she became intoxicated he took her to a common lodging house in George Street, partially undressed her and attempted to cut her throat. She struggled and screamed. However, her assailant ran off before he could be detained. The victim was able to give an excellent description of the man to the police, though he was never arrested.

The eighth Whitechapel murder took place on 20 December 1888 in Clark's Yard, High Street, Poplar, and was of Rose Mylett or Millett, a local prostitute, otherwise known as Lizzie Davis. There were no obvious marks of violence on the body and at first it was thought she had died suddenly from natural causes. Closer medical examination revealed that death was due to strangulation, a discovery which surprised the police, who would have expected ligature marks on the throat and neck, a protruding tongue and bulging eyes, as well as signs of a struggle at the site of the murder. The body was not otherwise interfered with. Indeed, debate continued for some time whether this was in fact a murder at all.

London had to wait until 17 July 1889 for the ninth murder. The victim was Alice McKenzie, aged forty, the partner of one John McCormack of Gun Street, Spitalfields. She was in the habit of going out at night, possibly for work as a prostitute, and was murdered in Castle Alley, Spitalfields. She was found with her throat cut, her clothes up to her waist, and wearing no drawers (this was not unusual for the time). Her genitals and her stomach were exposed and slashed across. A clay pipe and a farthing were found beside the body, but the 1s 8d her partner had given her that night as she went out was not to be found. The motive for the killing may have been sexual, although the body had not been badly mutilated; on the other hand it may have been a murder in the furtherance of robbery.

On 10 September 1889 the torso of an unknown woman was found under a railway arch in Pinchin Street, St George's-in-the-East. The head had been removed with a neat right-handed cut, and both legs had also been 'jointed' with neat butchery cuts. The torso was naked and bundled into a bloodstained chemise. Her hands were neatly kept and her body was plump and well-nourished. There was a single superficial knife cut downwards from the sternum to the genitals, but her insides had not been removed. Post-mortem examination revealed normal, healthy internal organs and no signs of recent coitus. The identity of the woman remains unknown, and in a number of particulars the crime did not appear to resemble the work of the Ripper.

The tenth and final murder in the Whitechapel killings series took place on 13 February 1891 in Swallow Gardens, Royal Mint Street, where Frances Coles, twenty-six years old and a prostitute, was attacked and killed by having her throat cut twice. Her body was not mutilated in any other way. The police constable who found her believed he saw a movement of her eyelids, and from the fact that the body was still warm and the blood still flowing, believed he may have interrupted her murderer in the course of his work, though in fact he saw no assailant. Medical examiners could detect no similarity with the work of the Ripper. A former seaman, Tom Saddler, a known associate of the dead woman, was examined closely as a possible suspect, particularly regarding his ownership of a knife, but was eventually discharged.

Why did the Ripper murders create such a sensation in London in the late 1880s, and how is it that the mystery was never solved? Part of the reason for the enormous interest taken in the killings was the gruesome detail in which the newly important popular press depicted the horrific anatomical circumstances of this string of crimes. The lower classes of London, in spite of their reputation for violence and disorder, were conventional and blinkered in their outlook, timid and easily frightened by the new horror in their midst, and the press, on the pretext of keeping them informed, played on this fearfulness with considerable skill. Rumour, innuendo, hatred of immigrant foreigners and hostility towards the East End's large and clearly recognisable Jewish community all added to fears which sprang mainly from insularity and ignorance. The crimes, too, reached down into their own number and seemed to threaten the lower orders themselves. Hysteria was never very far below the surface of the public reaction.

The 'Dear Boss' letters made this inflammable situation worse. Written in derisive tones, the first, composed in red ink on 25 September, struck a chilling note of threat for the working-class woman in the street:

> I am down on whores and shant quit ripping them till I do get buckled. Grand work the last lot was, I gave the lady no time to squeal. How can they catch me now, I love my work and want to start again. You will soon hear of me with my funny little games. I saved some of the proper red stuff in a ginger beer bottle over the last job to write with but it went thick like glue and I cant use it. Red ink is fit enough I hope ha ha.

Another 'Dear Boss' communication – a postcard, also addressed to the Central News Office – followed that same evening. Referring to a popular postcard which first appeared on the news stands on 1 October, it originated from 'Saucy Jacky' and described the Stride and Eddowes murders as the 'double event'. It said:

> I wasn't codding dear old Boss when I gave you the tip. You'll hear about Saucy Jacky's work tomorrow

double event this time number one squealed a bit couldn't finish straight off. Had no time to get the ears for the police.

The letters continued sporadically until as late as 1896, though they were not all in the same hand and their tone varied widely, as can be seen from this one of 5 October 1888:

Dear Friend, In the name of God hear me I swear I did not kill the female whose body was found at Whitehall. If she was an honest woman I will hunt down and destroy her murderer. If she was a whore God will bless the hand that slew her, for the women of Moab and Midian shall die and their blood shall mingle with the dust.

So punctual and well informed were the bulk of the letters that J.G. Littlechild, Chief Inspector of the Special Branch, believed they were written by Tom Bullen of the Central News Agency himself, and called it 'a smart piece of journalistic work'. Nevertheless the correspondence was given general credence by the public and added to the hysteria.

The fact that the Metropolitan Police arrested and carefully examined over 100 suspects before dropping the charges against them is much more a tribute to their fair-mindedness and impartiality than it is a criticism of their efficiency. In the conditions prevailing it would have been a simple task to fit somebody up with the murders; the fact that the police did not do so in spite of all the criticism directed against them meant that they were genuinely seeking the real culprit. The accused persons included a number of locally employed slaughtermen, several sailors ashore from the Pool of London and frequenting the East End, a miscellany of foreigners from as far afield as Australia and Canada, an unemployed German butcher called John Pizer ('Leather Apron') who was later detained in Bow Asylum as insane, an itinerant pedlar called McKenna, a mysterious Japanese, a homicidal tailor, another German immigrant called Ludwig who was given to violence and handy with a knife, a drunken medical student by the name of Bull, a vagrant called Packer who was arrested in Boulogne, a Swede by the name of Benelius who was a traveller, a Polish Jew called Isaacs, a former convict named Brodie who confessed to all the murders, and a religious maniac called Wentworth Bell Smith who was obsessed with fallen women and wrote voluminously about them.

At the beginning of 1894 M.L. Macnaghten, Chief Commissioner of Police, in a report denying an article that had appeared recently in the *Sun* that the murders had been committed by a newly released lunatic called Thomas Hayne Cutbush, set out his own list of three suspects 'likely to have committed this series of murders', all quite different from the above. They were: M.J. Druitt, a man of good family and a qualified doctor who was 'sexually insane' and committed suicide by jumping into the Thames at the end of December 1888; a Polish Jew by the name of Kominski, insane 'owing to many years indulgence in solitary vices', who had a strong hatred of prostitutes and marked homicidal tendencies; and Michael Ostrog, a Russian doctor and a convict who was a homicidal maniac and was subsequently detained in an asylum. Of these three, at the present time it is Dr Druitt who is most favoured by committed 'Ripperologists' as the author of the crimes (not least because the murders most often attributed to the Ripper ceased with his death). However, not a single one of these suspects was ever proceeded against.

Why was this? Much of the explanation lies in the very haphazard and unscientific police methods of the time. It is true that in September 1888 for the first time the police offered a reward of £100 to those bringing information leading to an arrest in the Ripper cases (though this was against strict Home Office guidelines), and in October sanctioned the use of bloodhounds in the search for the killer. In November they even took the extraordinarily far-sighted and progressive step of commissioning a Dr Thomas Bond to construct a psychological profile of the serial murderer they were hunting. But generally their level of professional competence was low. It was hampered by a vast mass of apparently pointless bureaucracy. Police paperwork was handwritten and was scruffy, ill-educated and often almost totally illegible. It circulated slowly and haphazardly, frequently finishing up on the wrong desk or getting lost altogether. Typed work was only just being introduced and for some reason was regarded by some superior officers as unacceptable. Procedures at scenes of crime were lax and disorganised; the responsibilities of officers were ill-defined; items of evidence were often lost or mislaid; methods of apprehending and interrogating suspects were generally pretty crude. Police photography and fingerprinting were in their infancy; blood-grouping was a thing of the future; and DNA testing would not be developed for a further hundred years. In the light of these shortcomings it is perhaps surprising that anything was ever achieved at all, or that police morale remained as high as it did. It would have been more surprising if such methods had ever been capable of solving the mystery of Jack the Ripper.

WAS THERE CANNIBALISM IN THE WILD WEST?

Stories are sometimes told of the practice of cannibalism in the trackless wastes of the western plains of the United States in the years of white settlement. People repeated tales of these grim occurrences, like the traditional ghost stories with which the settlers frightened and entertained themselves. Whether the inspiration for these stories was conjured out of the strange, vast emptiness of the plains, or whether from the malign spirits of the primitive native American tribesmen who had once roamed them, no one knows for certain. Occasionally, however, they seem to have had at least some historical foundation.

In the late spring of 1874 Alfred Packer, who had set out in the early months of the year with four companions on a gold-prospecting expedition in the Colorado Rockies, staggered into the Indian encampment at Los Pinos in the south-west corner of the state not far from the boundary with New Mexico. He was alone. Barefoot, ragged and filthy, he took refuge with the Ute tribe whose leader, Chief Ouray, regarded him with some suspicion. Not only did Packer have a considerable sum of money on him, but he seemed too well nourished to be starving. Originally he claimed to know little about the fate of his four companions. At first his story was that he had lost touch with them as the result of snow-blindness, but he was vague about whether he had become lost by accident or had been abandoned by his friends. He had wandered, he said, for some months, lost and destitute, in the almost uninhabited and desolate San Juan mountains. Chief Ouray looked at him quizzically and said of his story, 'You too damn fat.'

Packer was a veteran of the Civil War and at the age of thirty-one had set off with his four companions eastwards from Provo near Salt Lake City in Utah towards Denver in eastern Colorado, about 300 miles distant. Their objective was the gold fields of Breckenridge where the pickings were supposed to be rich. The party had somehow wandered into the San Juan range about 100 miles south of their intended path and had stumbled about for some time in savage blizzards, trying to regain their bearings. Their meagre supplies had soon run out, and after eating their horse's barley, they had been forced to consume the animal itself and even to attempt to eat its saddle. Then they turned on each other.

The first to go was sixty-year-old Israel Swann who died naturally from starvation. The others decided after a brief discussion to eat his corpse. Two more, James Humphry and Frank Miller, were also cooked and eaten after they died or were killed. Then Packer shot and killed his one remaining companion, Shannon Bell, claiming at first that Bell had gone berserk and attacked him with a hatchet, but later changing his story, alleging that he had returned from a scouting trip to find the other gnawing at the partly cooked limb of one of the party and had killed him in self-defence when Bell suddenly set upon him. He denied strongly that he had been involved in any other killings.

An expedition to the area some months later turned up the partly dismembered bodies of Packer's fellow prospectors, and he was arraigned on a charge of multiple murder. He was convicted and sentenced to hang, but the sentence was later commuted to one of life imprisonment on account of a technical fault in the indictment. He served seventeen years of his sentence and was released in 1891. He was later employed as a doorman in the offices of the *Denver Post*. Something of a local celebrity, he continued to protest his innocence to the end of his days in 1907.

The whole affair created one of the great mysteries of the American West, generating folklore, a number of songs and many gruesome jokes. Since Packer was the only survivor of the affair, it seems likely that the real truth will never be known. However, he was almost certainly guilty, if not of murder, at least of cannibalism, though this undoubtedly was the result of his extremely desperate situation. The evidence of murder produced against him at his trial seemed mostly to be circumstantial and hinged largely on the fact that when he made contact with the Ute he had in his possession a skinning knife and a money draft belonging to one of the others, drawn on Wells Fargo for a considerable sum. He was said to have made a sort of confession in the course of the investigation, but this was retracted at the time of his trial. It seemed likely to the court that he had made up the story of his quarrel with Shannon Bell as an extenuation of his misdeeds. If his story were true, however, and he had killed only one of the party, and that in self-defence, perhaps his acquittal on a capital charge was appropriate, since the crime of eating his dead companions might have been regarded even then as a lesser offence than murdering and consuming them.

THE EXTRAORDINARY CASE OF DR CRIPPEN

Most people have heard the gruesome details relating to Dr Crippen's murder of his wife in London in 1910. Even schoolchildren have read in their history textbooks how wireless (as radio was then known) played one of its early roles in his interception and arrest while he was fleeing to America with his lover, who was disguised as a boy. The basic facts have become part of the popular folklore of Edwardian England.

Hawley Harvey Crippen was born in Coldwater, Michigan, in 1862, his father a dealer in 'dry goods' (drapery and similar materials, so called to distinguish them from groceries). Having received a general education at California University, Michigan, he went on to study medicine at the Hospital College of Cleveland, Ohio. Later he took a diploma in ear and eye care in London, after which he returned to New York in 1895 and began selling patent medicines for a living. He had been married once already but now he fell in love with an ambitious and beautiful woman whom he knew as Cora Turner, but whom he later discovered was Kunigunde Mackamotzki, the daughter of a Russian-Polish immigrant father and a German mother. She entertained the ambition of becoming an operatic singer, but her singing voice, though sweet, was never very strong; and, though she attempted to find work as a music-hall artiste under the name of Belle Elmore, she was never successful in getting regular stage engagements. Partly as a result of her natural extravagance and partly because of her flirtatious behaviour she proved something of a trial to her mousy, undistinguished husband.

In 1900 Crippen, calling himself 'Doctor', moved with her to England and eventually took a house off the Camden Road, in Holloway, north London. He practised dentistry at a joint practice at Albion Chambers in New Oxford Street, and also became manager of a London patent medicine firm known as Munyon's Remedies. In 1907 he met and fell in love with Ethel le Neve, a typist in her early twenties, and an unassuming, pretty young woman, who was secretary to the medicine company. She seemed to Crippen to be everything his wife was not. Cora, with her raucous New York twang, was always spending money and splashing out on fancy dresses far beyond Crippen's means. She had several times threatened to leave him for her current lover ('with all her money', she said, although, of course, it was really her husband's since she had never earned a penny). On one occasion she had actually packed several trunks with her belongings and had them removed from the house at 39 Hilldrop Crescent to frighten him.

Outwardly their marital relations seemed above reproach, though there were a number of their acquaintances who suspected that all was not well in the household. Visitors observed that while Cora behaved extravagantly and accumulated personal luxuries as if she really were a star of the stage, at the same time she was extremely parsimonious in household spending. She always bought the cheapest cuts of meat at the market, and was slovenly and lazy as a wife, forcing Crippen to do more than his share of chores. In January 1910, thoroughly fed up with her, he bought five grains of hyoscine hydrobromide from a chemist's. On the 31st he hosted one of his wife's numerous evening parties in his home. After this soirée Cora Crippen was never seen alive again.

At his trial it was confidently asserted that Crippen had used the hyoscine to poison his wife. Then he cut up her body and burned the bones, perhaps in the kitchen stove; and having removed the portions of flesh that could have betrayed her identity (or even her sex), he destroyed them, burying the remainder in the cellar. This was a lengthy and exhausting process for a man who was not particularly strong, and hence it took some little time to accomplish.

Ethel le Neve was then invited to go to live with him at Hilldrop Crescent, moving in at the beginning of March. Crippen was said to have kept his dead wife's head all this time, concealed in a holdall, and to have disposed of it by dropping it in the Channel from the ferry when he and Ethel made an Easter trip to Dieppe at the end of that month. The couple had already given in their three-month notice to the landlord and declared their intention of leaving the country when their tenancy expired.

The interest of neighbours had been speedily aroused by Cora's disappearance and le Neve's arrival. Gossip among them brought a visit from the police in June. Two Scotland Yard detectives, Inspector Dew and Sergeant Mitchell, went to Hilldrop Crescent to question Crippen. A letter containing Cora's resignation from the Music Hall Ladies' Guild had already been received, written by Crippen himself, and during February and March he had made various visits to the pawnbrokers, raising substantial sums on items of his wife's personal jewellery. He also had upwards of £600 lodged at the Charing Cross Bank, most of it in the joint names of H.H. and Cora Crippen. At first he persisted with the story that his wife had left him and gone to California where she had died. He even inserted her obituary in the theatrical periodical, *The Era*, and sent telegrams to her friends telling them of her death. Later, under police questioning, he admitted that he had invented the story of her visit to California, her illness and her death. He now said that his wife had gone to Chicago with her lover, and that she was still living there – though he did not have her address. The police, their suspicions now thoroughly aroused, embarked seriously on their task of investigating the case. They even secured Crippen's permission to search the house at Hilldrop Crescent for evidence.

In early July Crippen and Ethel le Neve left London suddenly for the Continent. A few days later their descriptions were circulated by the police, who wanted them for further questioning. Only a few days afterwards human remains were discovered in the cellar of the house in Hilldrop Crescent and the police issued warrants for the arrest of Crippen and le Neve. On 20 July Crippen and his young mistress joined the Canadian Pacific liner SS *Montrose* at Antwerp, sailing for Canada.

Captain Kendall, the liner's master, became suspicious of the close and affectionate relationship between two of his passengers, a Mr Robinson and his son, who had boarded at Antwerp bound for Quebec and whom he had observed holding hands. The couple were Dr Crippen and Ethel le Neve. She was disguised as a boy in a suit of juvenile clothing specially bought for her by Crippen in London, a purchase which until then had very much puzzled the police. The captain sent a wireless message to Scotland Yard alerting the police to his suspicions (this being the first time that wireless was employed to track down a criminal), and the two stalwart policemen were sent on a faster ship, the *Laurentic*, which overhauled the *Montrose* and took the couple off at Father Point before they could land at Quebec. They arrived back in Liverpool and were committed at Bow Street for trial at the Old Bailey.

Their cases opened separately in October, he on a charge of wilful murder, she accused of being his accomplice. Crippen was tried before the Lord Chief Justice, Lord Alverstone, defended by the barrister A.A. Tobin (with Huntley Jenkins and a Mr Roome as juniors) and with R.D. Muir leading the prosecution, the case opening on 8 October. After an extensively reported trial lasting five days the jury brought in a verdict of guilty on Crippen. Ethel le Neve, defended by F.E. Smith (later Lord Birkenhead), was acquitted and released. After his conviction, Crippen appealed to the Court of Criminal Appeal, but his plea was dismissed and he was hanged at Pentonville on 23 November 1910. No voice was raised against the verdict, and most people remained convinced that Crippen had been rightly convicted of a vicious and unusually brutal killing. Yet there were some features of the case that were quite extraordinary.

The first was the extremely vociferous part played in the case by the popular press. Aided by the wide spread of literacy after the Forster Education Act of

1870 and the stress this act had laid on what were often called the 'three Rs' (writing, reading and arithmetic), there was now a very big demand among the working classes for cheap and simple reading matter; and this demand the penny and the halfpenny papers, with their new steam-operated rotary presses, sought to fulfil. Chief among the publications covering the case were the *Daily Mail* and the *Daily Mirror*, which pumped out endless columns retailing a good deal of gossip and rumour, as well as many of the sensational facts of the murder. They took profit from supplying the reading public with all the salacious details, no feature of the Crippens' domestic scene being too small to relate. During the Atlantic chase, they published daily front-page maps indicating the progress of the *Montrose* and the *Laurentic* in their pursuit of the fugitives, and after their capture left no stone unturned in their quest to blacken Crippen's name. At the trial they commented freely on Crippen's quiet, withdrawn manner, noting that he remained unperturbed even when there was court discussion of whether the crease in a piece of exhumed flesh was an operation scar, as the prosecution maintained, or whether it was, as the defence believed, merely a fold in her skin. He did not even react when portions of the flesh were passed round the jury in a soup plate for them to examine. By their merciless and often fanciful observations, the press went a long way towards convicting the accused before any verdict was given.

With the unprecedentedly high degree of public interest in the case, the newspapers had no wish to see this exciting story brought to an end. Large sums of money – sometimes as much as £100 – were offered to those with stories to tell. The egregious proprietor of

John Bull, Horatio Bottomley, put up money to help finance Crippen's defence in the hope of some subsequent profit on the case. This was an early and vivid illustration of the need for some kind of formal regulation to curtail press abuses of the sort.

A second problem about the case was the strange choice of hyoscine as a poison. With his knowledge of pharmaceutics Crippen could have chosen many better ways of destroying his wife if he had desired, since traces of hyoscine would remain detectable for long periods after their administration. Crippen's explanation for the use of this drug was that Cora had unusually vigorous sexual appetites which he found difficult to fulfil (especially in view of his new commitments to Ethel), and his knowledge of the drug had informed him of its use as a sexual depressant in cases of acute nymphomania. Thus an element of black comedy entered this dreadful trial, with the portrait of the murderer using a deadly remedy so as to restrain his wife's uncontrollable sexual urges. He maintained he had only given her a minimal dose, well diluted in the appropriate quantity of water. Unfortunately he was unable to account for what had happened to the rest of the five grains he had bought, though he felt rather vaguely it must have been used in some other case, perhaps in relation to his dentistry. Certainly none of his purchase remained to be produced, and the jury found it hard to believe that a person trained in the use of drugs could have administered such a lethal overdose by accident.

A third odd feature of the case was Crippen's readiness to have the house searched and his equanimity over the police suggestion that they excavate the cellar. The police had taken his statement in a visit to Albion Chambers, when Crippen fitted in their interview between dental appointments. They admitted that Crippen remained always cool, equable in temper and cooperative in his attitude, showing not the least sign of panic or confusion even when they were searching his home. He seemed sure that they would not find anything, and yet, in his absence, when Inspector Dew dug up the bricks that formed the cellar floor, part of the bundles of flesh the police found there were buried in what they claimed was one of Crippen's old pyjama jackets (a claim the defence strongly denied). If he was bluffing when he assured the police that he was hiding nothing, it was an extraordinarily risky gamble he was making.

The eminent criminal advocate Sir Edward Marshall Hall later took the view that Crippen was badly defended in court, and that if he had been conducting the case he could have got the charge reduced to one of manslaughter. There is in fact little evidence that the case was mishandled, though a review of the proceedings tends to show that the defence did not always make its points as strongly as it might have. Take a single example of this. During his tenancy of the house in Hilldrop Crescent, Crippen had paid a short visit to the United States, only to find on his return that Cora had taken up quite publicly with a Mr Bruce Miller, with whose enjoyable attentions she taunted Crippen. The defence said that the episode was typical of his wife's infidelity. Miller, now living in East Chicago, Indiana, with a wife and their child, was cited to appear, and, while admitting to the court certain improprieties in their relationship, swore that he had never done more than kiss her, and said with perfect truth and candour that he had not run away with her.

Crippen was unable to summon the real abductor, since he did not know who he was; but the court was left with the unfortunate impression that Crippen was making the whole story up.

The case was also complicated by serious confusion among the expert witnesses as to the significance to be attached to the gruesome remains unearthed in the cellar. There was little doubt that these were of human origin, but in their existing condition it was almost impossible to say with any certainty what part of the body they came from. Some of the doctors believed they came from the upper thigh; others from the stomach, where Cora was supposed to bear a scar after an operation to remove her ovaries. There was even doubt as to whether they came from Mrs Crippen at all. The defence made some play with the logical impossibility of convicting a man if the victim turned out not to be his missing wife; but before the invention of modern biological procedures such as DNA testing it was impossible to be sure. A number of medical witnesses – including Bernard (afterwards Sir Bernard) Spilsbury, later a distinguished forensic pathologist – gave evidence, but what they said left the judge in a state of confused exasperation.

There is one further damaging omission in the case against Crippen. After his conviction for murder a letter was received from the USA purporting to have been written in her self-imposed exile by Cora Crippen herself and pleading for mercy for her long-suffering husband. This letter was examined by the police and passed to the prosecution, at least one of whose graphologists, on the strength of the way she wrote the letter y, confirmed that it was indeed in Cora's handwriting. Quite improperly, however, the existence of the letter was not made known to the defence team. It was passed up to the Home Secretary of the time, Winston Churchill, who simply stuffed it into his pocket and said no more about it. It seems very likely that if the defence lawyers or the Court of Appeal had known about the existence of such a letter there would have been at least a stay of execution, if not a late reprieve of the unfortunate doctor.

The startling possibility remains, therefore, that Mrs Crippen may not have been murdered at all. She must have been mystified that her dramatic letter, so vital to her husband's defence, remained unanswered; worse still, that in spite of it, he was hanged. But this, of course, cannot be entirely the end of the matter. If the body buried in the cellar in Hilldrop Crescent, allegedly in Crippen's pyjama jacket, was not that of Cora Crippen, whose was it, and who put it there?

AMERICAN GANGSTERISM AND THE ST VALENTINE'S DAY MASSACRE

The activities of armed American gangsters in Chicago during the late 1920s, and in particular the episode known as the St Valentine's Day Massacre, are well known both to students of American social history and to devotees of Hollywood films. Less frequently discussed is the question of why so little progress was made in the police investigation and suppression of these gangs.

The feud between two of the most influential city gangs – those led by Alphonse (Al) Capone and George

(Bugs) Moran – was fuelled during the era of
Prohibition (1919–33) by rivalry for the control of the
illegal traffic in alcohol and the running of 'speak-
easies', betting firms, gambling saloons, innumerable
brothels and various 'protection' empires. It reached a
gruesome peak when seven members of the Moran
gang were machine-gunned to death at their HQ in a
garage in North Clark Street, downtown Chicago, on a
bleak February morning in 1929.

Byron Bolton, a former expert machine-gunner from
the US Navy, was reported in 1934 as having confessed
to leading six others in committing the outrage. Their
stories were widely reported in the local and national
press. Two of their number were said to have mas-
queraded as policemen, disarmed the victims, and
lined them up facing the garage wall. Then others of
the group appeared and in a few seconds mercilessly
gunned down Moran's men. The victims were three ex-
convicts working for Moran – Peter and Frank
Gusenberg and Arthur Hayes; James Clark, brother of
Bugs Moran and one of the North Side gang leaders at
the time; and two other gang members called Albert
Weinschank and Reinhart Schwimmer. The seventh
victim was one John May, a car mechanic and an
employee of the garage who had the misfortune to be
present at the time. Bolton's story traced the massacre
to the ambitions of the New York gangster Frank Uale,
who was said to have challenged Capone for a 'piece'
of a dog-track operating in Lyons, Illinois, and who
was working with the Moran gang to secure it. The
crime, the most brutal in Chicago annals, shocked the
whole nation. Yet no police prosecution was ever
brought against the perpetrators of the outrage, and the
bungling incompetence, obsessive secrecy, paralytic

delays, institutional bureaucracy and even the plain crookedness of the US police at the time almost beggar belief. How did the American police contrive to fumble such an obvious catch?

One reason for this sorry tale undoubtedly springs from the constitutional division of responsibility between the federal government and those of the states. The Federal Bureau of Investigation (FBI) together with its agents (the 'G-men' or 'government men' employed in its work) and the state police authorities, in this case the Chicago Police Department (the CPD), were the two parties in this story. The state police were as sensitive of what they saw as bureau superciliousness as they were anxious to preserve their department from federal encroachment. There were strictly drawn and rigid lines of legal demarcation between state and federal bodies, and this often made for inter-departmental friction rather than smooth cooperation. The CPD undertook an inquiry into the massacre, but had difficulty in finding evidence, partly because nobody seemed willing to talk and partly because of the not inconsiderable number of police officers and other legal officials whom Capone had on his payroll (it was reckoned that a corrupt law enforcement officer, depending on his rank, could pull in up to $5,000 a week in addition to his normal salary). The state police had taken possession of hundreds of cartridges picked up from the garage floor for forensic investigation but failed to make anything of them, chiefly because they had no forensic laboratory in which the cartridges could be properly examined. The FBI, apart from being less susceptible to local corruption, did possess such specialist laboratory services both for ballistics and for fingerprinting, but held aloof from the case chiefly on the grounds that, since no violation of federal law had taken place (murder was not a federal offence), they lacked the competence that would have enabled them to institute their enquiries. Hence in 1929 no progress was made in the police investigation and no one was arrested.

The second reason for the failure to bring anyone to justice for the St Valentine's Day massacre was the quite impenetrable shroud of secrecy under which the FBI operated. They not only refused to talk to the newspapers and the general public, instead hitting enquiries as far as they could into the long grass; they also remained utterly uncommunicative with the state police, refusing to answer even routine questions. Indeed, in some cases they would not even talk to each other. Their press releases are littered with phrases such as: 'I have no knowledge of the matter mentioned' and 'Bolton made no such statement concerning the affair'. Yet there exist very specific secret memoranda in which J. Edgar Hoover (the bureau boss), his staff and the Department of Justice show considerable familiarity with the details of the whole case. Furthermore, the bureau was perfectly aware that it was concealing masses of important information, as can be seen from the elaborate enquiries instituted in its offices into the possibility of phone taps. It even encouraged the filing of phoney evidence in the bureau so as to discover which official was leaking it and which newspaper picked up the misinformation first. The intention often seemed to be the concealment rather than the investigation of the whole affair.

Press reporting was the third reason for the confusion surrounding the case. Wide sections of the US press took a lively interest in the case and reported it to the best of their ability. The papers published grim photographs and gruelling descriptions of the murder scene, telling how the greasy walls of the garage were spattered with gobbets of flesh, with pools of blood trickling down into the drain in the floor; how all the victims were shot to pieces by the noisy blast of 500 rounds per minute from the tommy-guns, all of them dead except one who succumbed shortly afterwards. They related how a ground-floor room opposite the garage in North Clark Street had been rented for several days by Byron Bolton to watch out for the gang's arrival, and how the state police had found an envelope addressed to Bolton there. They had followed up the postmark to Thayer, Illinois, had located Bolton's parents in the locality and had obtained a photo which was then identified by the woman who had rented him the room. The newspaper accounts were so similar that the reader could be forgiven for thinking they had copied from each other. But there were some differences. For one thing, the number and type of machine-guns employed varied from one account to another: one story said two tommy-guns had been used, another that it was four. Indeed, one FBI report stated that the weapon was a heavy machine-gun mounted on a stand and disguised as a camera. Other differences occurred over the role attributed to Frank Uale, whom they had presented as in alliance with Bugs Moran and who was therefore eliminated by Al Capone to preserve his own empire. This could not have been true since Uale was killed in New York in early July 1928, long before the massacre took place. Furthermore, the names of the persons fingered by Bolton as his accomplices were not the same in the newspapers as in police files: three appeared in both – Fred (Killer) Burke, Gus Winkler and Fred Goetz (known as 'the Brain' because he claimed to have a degree from Illinois University) – but there was doubt about the others. Bolton named them as Claude Maddox and Murray Humphreys, at one time Capone's number one gunman, but police believed them to be Robert Conroy (alias Robert Newberry) and Bolton's own brother John. Bolton later changed his story, saying that the two extra men were Ray Nugent and Bob Carey, and that Maddox had only been involved as the man who afterwards abandoned and burned the Cadillac used for the crime. It began to appear as if Bolton was using his list of names in pursuit of some unknown personal agenda.

None of the above information became public knowledge until 1935 when Bolton was arrested on a raid in Chicago in connection with other offences and made his confession. His motives seem to have been various: to protect his criminal associates (and his own brother); to gain immunity from punishment by 'singing' (betraying his partners); and to cover his back by putting forward dummy names – three on his list had perished in gangland wars, two were serving life terms in state penitentiaries, and only one, Maddox, was still at large.

The CPD were naturally keen to establish that it was at Al Capone's wishes, if not on his actual orders, that the massacre had been carried out, since they already had Capone imprisoned in Alcatraz on a charge of tax evasion and would very much have liked to convict him for multiple murder and send him to the electric chair; but this did not prove easy. The FBI were, as usual, unhelpful and seemed to have other fish to fry.

Claude Maddox was apprehended at the end of January 1935. The accusation against him had the ring of truth, since he was well known as a get-away driver and as a member of the Circus gang (named after the city café in which they met) who were familiar as small-time associates of the Capone outfit. However, Maddox was contemptuous of the charge and had no difficulty in proving his innocence since he was actually in court facing another charge at the time the massacre took place. The CPD kept him behind bars as long as they could without an actual conviction and declared him a 'public enemy', but they lacked the evidence to bring him to court and had to let him go.

So, at the end of the day, no one was ever brought to justice for one of America's most notorious gangland killings. Though Prohibition had ended in 1933, Capone's Chicago empire flourished as vigorously as ever under his cousin Francesco Raffaele Nitto, known as Frank Nitti and nicknamed 'the Enforcer'. Dealing in betting, gambling, prostitution and protection, the empire at its peak was valued at around $100 million.

Al Capone was released from Alcatraz on grounds of ill health in 1939 but never regained his footing in Chicago. He died in penurious obscurity in Florida in 1947.

4

Plots and Intrigues

THE GUNPOWDER PLOT: WAS ITS DISCOVERY A MIRACULOUS DELIVERANCE?

In early November 1605 London, and later the rest of England, was to hear the most blood-curdling news. Since the story came from official pronouncements by the government there was, it seemed, no reason to disbelieve any of it, fantastically improbable although it might be. It appeared that at around midnight on 4/5 November a search party inspecting the storeroom beneath the House of Lords discovered a miscreant calling himself John Johnson (later to be identified as Guy or Guido Fawkes) who was busy laying fuses to a huge quantity of gunpowder. On 5 November Parliament was due to be opened. Had Johnson not been discovered, and had he succeeded in lighting the fuses a few hours later, the House of Lords would have been obliterated in a mighty explosion. For the opening of the new session of Parliament not only the Lords but also the Commons would have been gathered together in the same chamber to hear the king's speech, and in the galleries there would have been noble wives and such of the king's and nobility's children as were mature enough to attend. The whole ruling class of England would have been wiped out in one blow.

Waiting in the wings were the Roman Catholic plotters, wanting to set up a puppet monarchy with such of the royal children as survived, or even with King James's cousin Arabella Stuart on the throne. Once the Roman Catholics seized power the Catholic Terror would, it was commonly believed, have been far worse than any remembered from the days of Mary Tudor. The Church of England would have been proscribed and the Inquisition would have spread its deadly tentacles throughout the land. England would once more have been in grave danger of becoming a province of Spain. No wonder that even on the day of discovery the government encouraged the people of London to celebrate Parliament's lucky escape by lighting bonfires. Had it not been for the last-minute intervention of divine providence all would have been lost. This appeared to be a highly dramatic and deeply sinister crisis, threatening the whole future of the nation. But was this presentation of the Gunpowder Plot in fact the true one?

Some nineteenth-century Roman Catholic historians asserted that there was no Gunpowder Plot at all, that it was all a fictional propaganda exercise by the government and that the plotters were innocent of the crimes for which they suffered a terrible death. But there certainly was a plot. On 20 May 1604 Robert (Robin) Catesby and four others – Thomas Wintour, Robert Wintour, Thomas Percy and Guy Fawkes – met in the Duck and Drake Inn, near the Strand, and there Catesby proposed the destruction by gunpowder of king and Parliament for the furtherance of the Catholic cause. Catesby was an extremist and Fawkes was a soldier of fortune, but they and other more moderate Roman Catholics had good reason to feel bitter against both king and Parliament. While James I had been only James VI of Scotland, his claim to the English throne had not been universally acknowledged. In an endeavour to win the support of English Catholics James had made verbal (but not written) promises to mitigate the penal laws against them in England, and indeed at the outset of his English reign recusancy fines against Catholics for non-attendance at Church of England services had been remitted. James's own conversion to Catholicism had been widely rumoured. After all James's Lutheran wife, Anne of Denmark, had converted just before 1600, and James had taken a very tolerant attitude to her new faith. But Catholic hopes were soon to be dashed. Advised by his new chief minister, Robert Cecil, Earl of Salisbury, James negotiated peace with Spain but set his face against Spanish efforts to secure religious toleration.

The king dashed Presbyterian hopes at the Hampton Court Conference in 1604, proclaiming 'no bishops, no king'; but he also appreciated the dangers of encouraging a Roman Catholic revival in England and therefore he gave his support to parliamentary proposals to tighten anti-Catholic legislation, agreeing with some reluctance to the reimposition of recusancy fines. Cecil had no such reluctance. The Counter-Reformation was proceeding apace, and every year swathes of central Europe returned to the Old Faith. The Inquisition still randomly tortured Protestant seamen in Spanish ports. Religious toleration of a sort was only practised in countries such as France where it was a political necessity. Cecil saw Roman Catholicism as many saw Communism in the twentieth century – a threat not only to their way of life but to their very existence. He feared that if the laws against

Roman Catholics were relaxed many thousands would return to the Old Faith, and England could well be plunged into political and civil strife.

Some English Roman Catholics were prepared to do just that to the country. Unaware of the impending peace between England and Spain, Thomas Wintour and Guy Fawkes had found Spain unreceptive to their urgings for an invasion of England, where, the Spaniards were optimistically assured, much of the population was Catholic at heart and would rise to their support. In April 1604 Wintour and Fawkes returned from Spain disillusioned, and easily fell in with Catesby's breathtaking proposal.

It was perhaps fortunate for the plotters that fear of plague twice caused the postponement of Parliament's new session, for they would not have been ready. First it was necessary to acquire enough gunpowder to be certain that the explosion would decimate if not annihilate all those present at the opening. It used to be asserted that since the government had a monopoly of the gunpowder supply it must have been aware of the purchase of such a large quantity as thirty-six barrels. But the monopoly was always unenforceable. Most merchant ships carried gunpowder, gunsmiths sold it, mining required it, and since the war was over there was now a glut. Nevertheless, it took a long time to collect together so much, and some of it deteriorated and had to be replaced in August 1605.

The official account of the plot at first mentioned a tunnel whereby the plotters transported the gunpowder to the storeroom which they had hired under the House of Lords. But no trace of a tunnel was ever found, and the shoring up of its walls and the disposal of its excavated soil would surely have left some evidence. Guy Fawkes did not mention a tunnel during his first four interrogations. His mention of it during the fifth seems likely to have been made in response to harsh questioning and at that stage he would probably have been willing to admit to anything.

As the plotters intended to support the explosion with armed rebellion it was necessary to involve more sympathisers. But the more people in the know, the greater the danger of betrayal. At first they were only five, but the number grew to thirteen. And others must have had partial knowledge if not the full details; some of the wives would have known, and some hints were certainly dropped to priests during confession.

When the government first learned of the plot is by no means certain. Cecil's agents and spies were everywhere, and several of the thirteen were under suspicion and subject to surveillance. By the summer of 1605 the government must have been aware that something was afoot, although it did not know exactly what. It would be a tremendous coup for the government to allow the plot to ripen (Cecil's phrase) and to reveal it at the last desperate moment when the impact of the shock and horror it created would be most effective. And so it proved. On 26 October a mysterious letter was delivered under cover of darkness to Lord Monteagle, brother-in-law of Francis Tresham, one of the most recent recruits to the plot.

> My Lord, out of the love I bear to some of your friends, I have a care for your preservation. Therefore I would advise you as you tender your life, to devise some excuse to shift of your attendance at this Parliament. . . . For though there be no

appearance of any stir, yet I say they shall receive a terrible blow this Parliament; and yet they shall not see who hurts them. The danger is passed as soon as you have burnt this letter. . . .

Monteagle had some difficulty in deciphering the letter at first, but realising its importance, despite the lateness of the hour he decided to take it at once to Cecil. In the meantime Monteagle's servant, Thomas Ward, took the opportunity of his master's visit to Cecil to warn Catesby that the plotters were about to be betrayed. Catesby was certain at first that his cousin Tresham had written the letter, but was convinced by Tresham's protestations of denial. Nor did Tresham claim authorship several weeks later as he lay dying when to do so could well have mitigated the government's severity against his heirs. One of the wives may have been responsible for the document, but the choice of a letter rather than a quiet word in Monteagle's ear seems rather melodramatic and even dangerous; the spoken word leaves no trace, the written word is palpable evidence. Thomas Percy has also been suggested as the author of the note, but he would have been more likely to have reported it to his kinsman and employer, the Earl of Northumberland, who might have reacted to it with less undue haste than Monteagle and given the plotters some breathing space. The most likely scenario is that some days before 26 October Tresham gave Monteagle a warning sufficient to alert Cecil to the impending danger. How much information was passed on is uncertain but Cecil was confident enough to arrange for the Monteagle letter to be written and then to sit back and wait for developments.

The letter was thus an elaborate government fake intended by Cecil as a means of uncovering the plot which would exonerate Monteagle from his connection with it and would give the scheme a heightened air of mystery and suspense. Cecil did not show the letter to the king until 1 November, and despite James's urgings did not order a search of the storeroom until the opening of Parliament was only a few hours away. All the actions of the government suggest that it was in possession of the main outline of the plot as early as late October, although it did not know all the details or all the identities of those involved. Cecil wanted the country's deliverance to be as dramatic as possible. Only if he was in complete command of the situation would he have dared take the risk of allowing the plot to come so close to fruition.

Even so, the government was surprised to learn that the storeroom under the House of Lords had been hired by Northumberland's kinsman, Thomas Percy. A search party was sent to find and arrest him on 5 November. It was not until the evening of the 6th that the government was in possession of a number of other names. The list was confirmed by Fawkes, probably after he had been racked on 7 November. That Fawkes was gratuitously racked to extract and confirm names which the government already knew seems a strong possibility, for the administration issued a proclamation on that day naming a number of the plotters who were gathering in the Midlands. The men in question assembled at Holbeach House in Staffordshire late that evening. They knew already that their cause was hopeless; it seemed also cursed, for the wet gunpowder they were drying before the fire exploded, injuring several and blinding John Grant. Next day 200 men closed in on Holbeach and after a short and bloody encounter most of the defenders were taken prisoner; several, including Catesby, were killed.

In the aftermath of the plot the government issued its own version of events. It had no more interest in telling the truth than the surviving plotters, who would lie through their teeth and then agree to anything when racked. The horror of what Parliament and king had narrowly escaped was much played upon, yet when nearly a ton of recovered gunpowder was conveyed to the Tower it was officially described as 'decayed'. So there might after all have been no big bang. But the government wanted all England to believe the plot to be both real and diabolical. It now set about linking the plot to the Jesuits. A Father Garnet was condemned for his involvement because he had not revealed to the government the treasons he had learned of during the confessional.

The government did not quite succeed in blackening the whole body of English Catholics, the vast majority of whom would have recoiled in horror at what had been planned by their co-religionists. But the plot deterred James I from ameliorating the severe anti-Catholic laws, it dashed Anne of Denmark's hopes, and it forced Catholics to be even more private in their search for spiritual consolation. Catesby was the chief plotter, but from late October Cecil was the principal controller. He had known the main outline of the scheme and had hijacked it for a purpose. He wanted the narrowness of the escape and the horror of it to kill any reservations Englishmen might have about the impending anti-Catholic legislation, and he wanted James's brush with death to bring the king to heel. He also wanted to use the plot to discredit the Jesuits. So the Gunpowder Plot was as much an aspect of government policy as the peace with Spain, and the Monteagle letter was its instrument. It had long-term consequences too. Anti-Catholic fires and processions, with burnings of the effigy of the pope, continued well into the twentieth century, religious toleration notwithstanding. Roman Catholics had to wait over 200 years for the final removal of legal disabilities, and the anti-Catholic bias the Gunpowder Plot helped to consolidate was seen again during the Popish Plot in 1679 and at the settlement of the Protestant succession in 1701 and 1714.

Catesby, Fawkes and the others would probably never have succeeded; the risk of betrayal and the decayed gunpowder militated against them. Their legacy was rather different from what they had intended. But the plot was a triumph for the English government, both in its detection and in its consequences.

WHAT HAPPENED TO COUNT KÖNIGSMARCK?

There are many legends about George I of England. It was long believed that he could not speak a word of English. It is now known that he spoke the language passably well, if with a heavy German accent, and that he could write good idiomatic English, as is shown in his comments on cabinet papers. It has been said that soon after his accession he stopped attending cabinet meetings, yet there is evidence that he attended most, including one as late as 1723 for which the minutes exist. He was supposedly unattractive physically, yet this is not reflected in his portraits (even allowing for favourable artistic licence), nor in contemporary descriptions. He was slightly short, but he did not want for mistresses. Hostile critics have condemned his harsh treatment of his wife, Sophia Dorothea, after their divorce, but she was amply provided for; nor was her seclusion in the castle of Ahlden as rigorous as has often been supposed. But was George entirely uninvolved in the mysterious disappearance of Count Philipp Christoph von Königsmarck, his wife's lover, on 1 July 1694?

Georg Ludwig, son of the Duke of Brunswick-Lüneburg and Hanover, and great-grandson of James I of England, had little inkling during his childhood and early manhood of the English prize that was to become his as George I in 1714. In the early 1680s Charles II and from 1685 James II were quite capable of fathering an heir to the English throne. Anne, James's daughter, was remarkable for her fecundity; her last child was still alive in 1700. So it was German politics, not English hopes, that determined the choice of George's cousin, Sophia Dorothea of Celle, as his bride-to-be. The choice was, of course, made by his parents, Ernst August and Sophia, who intended the marriage to result in the eventual reunification of Brunswick-Celle and Brunswick-Lüneburg. Virtually all unions among the ruling classes were arranged and most were reasonably successful. There was no particular reason why this one should not be both fertile and harmonious. They were married in 1682 and the union was fertile enough: a boy,

George August (later George II of England), was born in 1683 and a daughter, Sophia Dorothea (given her mother's names), in 1687.

But the marriage was already under strain. George was absent from Hanover for long periods, either fighting the Turks at the siege of Vienna (1683) or attending to other military or diplomatic duties. Sophia Dorothea had little to interest her and soon became bored with her life, especially with her husband. George's response to his wife's indifference was to take a mistress, Melusine von der Schulenburg; Sophia Dorothea's response to her dull life was to liven it up with a lover, Philipp Christoph von Königsmarck. He was physically attractive, exciting and reckless; he was also ambitious, courageous and penniless. That he and Dorothea became lovers in the physical sense is beyond dispute, despite her subsequent denials; the proof lies in the voluminous correspondence between the two, more than half of which has survived.

They were introduced at court in 1688. By 1690 they were corresponding. They made no attempt to keep their liaison a secret, and soon they were under pressure to end it, both from Philipp's friends and from Dorothea's parents and parents-in-law. It was a very sensitive time for Hanover. In March 1693 the emperor had elevated Hanover to become the ninth electorate, an honour of little power but much dignity and precedence. The title had yet to be confirmed by the imperial Diet, and Ernst August, George's father, was anxious to avoid any breath of scandal which might offend the emperor and influence the Diet. Thus when it seemed clear in the early summer of 1694 that the lovers were planning to run off together and set up a separate establishment there was consternation in Hanoverian court circles.

Matters were brought to a head by Königsmarck's visit to Augustus of Saxony in June 1694. Augustus could not or would not pay off his gambling debt to Königsmarck but did offer him a regiment in the Saxon army. This would give Königsmarck a regular income and a reasonable measure of security. He would, of course, have to return to Hanover to resign his colonelcy in the Hanoverian army. At the same time Dorothea, who had been visiting her parents, returned to Hanover without making an expected call on the electress at Herrenhausen. She feigned illness and secluded herself in her private apartments. George, for some reason, chose this moment to visit his sister and brother-in-law in Berlin, so that at the crucial time he was well away from Hanover. Königsmarck, meanwhile, avoided his friends and neglected to resign his commission. This aroused the utmost suspicion at court, and Ernst August broke with summer tradition and returned hastily to Hanover. The couple were closely watched. On the evening of 1 July 1694 Königsmarck was observed entering the Leineschloss palace by a side door from which he made his way towards Dorothea's rooms. Whether he had been inveigled there by a forged note supposedly from Dorothea is immaterial; he had, in the preceding months, never missed any opportunity to visit her. But this visit was his last. He was never seen again.

From here on everything is speculation. Königsmarck's fate was kept secret for some time. When confronted with evidence of her liaison Dorothea happily agreed to a divorce, believing that Königsmarck was still alive. George was soon made aware of his wife's guilt but not of her lover's fate, although it is difficult to believe that he had set off for Berlin completely unaware of his wife's disloyalty which had been widely known for several years. It is likely that he knew a crisis was approaching when he consented to visit his sister, although he may not have been told exactly what was planned, or even if there were any exact plans. It may be that the intention was merely to arrest Königsmarck but that he died resisting arrest; it is more likely, however, that the plan was to silence him for good. The close involvement of George's father, the elector, and Königsmarck's enemy, the Countess von Platen, seems beyond dispute. Hanoverian and Celle sources put about various conflicting stories: that Königsmarck had been killed resisting arrest; that he had been allowed to escape abroad; that he had been murdered and his weighted body thrown into the Leine river; and even that his remains had been interred under the floorboards of a room in the Leineschloss. No remains were ever found.

Exactly what was done will never be known, but who did it can be identified with reasonable certainty. A Danish diplomat named four courtiers as the murderers: Nicolo Montalban, Wilken von Klenke, Johann von Stubenvol and Freiherr von Eltz. All were devoted and loyal servants of the elector. Their involvement is largely confirmed by the payment to Montalban, shortly after 1 July, of the first three-monthly instalment of a total sum 100 times the salary of the electorate's highest paid minister. The payment by instalments looks very much like hush-money. Two of the others subsequently rose high in the service of the elector. The Danish source says that the body of the victim, weighted with stones and chains and contained in a sack, was disposed of in the Leine. Königsmarck's relatives, Hanover's enemies, the king of Sweden and even the emperor did their utmost to get at the truth, but they were thwarted at every turn.

George only became fully aware of the extent of his wife's misconduct and the depth of her contempt for him when he read the Königsmarck–Dorothea correspondence, which came into his hands after her rooms were searched. Divorce was inevitable, partly because to continue the marriage would have been unendurable for them both, and partly to illegitimise any child of Königsmarck's that she might be bearing. George had to endure the divorce proceedings, but after this he froze at any mention of Dorothea's name and refused any discussion of the Königsmarck affair. Requests for him to relax the restrictions placed on Dorothea might have met a sympathetic ear – George was not a vindictive man and had made generous financial provision for her with only limited restrictions on her movements and access to her by others – but Dorothea soon became the object of political intrigue. Hanover's enemies took up her cause and from 1714 the Jacobite propagandists made much of her fate and her proclamations of innocence. It was undoubtedly a relief to George when she died in 1726, although he himself had only a few months longer to live. However, Jacobites and hostile historians have been unable to unearth any substantive evidence to involve him in Königsmarck's disappearance, and it seems most likely that he had been packed off to Berlin by his parents with little inkling of what was to come.

WAS GEORGE III REALLY MAD?

That George III was mad was long accepted as a commonplace of history. It was convenient for the Americans to be in rebellion against a tyrannical madman and it suited Whig historians to agree with their verdict. This old legend dies hard. Even today it stubbornly retains its place in historical folklore.

In the first week of November 1788 rumour swept London that King George III was deranged. He had not been seen in public for several weeks, and it was even reported that, since he had descended from his carriage in Windsor Great Park and addressed a tree as the King of Prussia, it had been necessary to keep him under restraint.

Rumour soon gave way to fact when the king's illness was reported to Parliament and a regency bill mooted. George was removed from Windsor to Kew where he was placed in the hands of physicians, the chief of whom was Dr Willis, renowned for his spectacular success with some of the inmates of Bedlam, London's hospital for the insane. From the first Dr Willis assured Prime Minister William Pitt that the king would recover fully; meanwhile, some of the other physicians assured Charles James Fox, the opposition leader, that recovery was unlikely. So from the outset the king's illness was of great political importance. If he recovered Pitt would remain in power; if he remained ill a regency would be necessary, and the regent, George's eldest son, would put Fox into office.

For nearly two centuries it was taken for granted that the king's illness was psychotic rather than physical;

after all, he raved like a madman and behaved like a madman. And this view was confirmed for many by the brilliance of Nigel Hawthorne's performance as George in Alan Bennett's play *The Madness of King George*. Hawthorne repeated his success in the title role when the play was turned into a film and reached a much wider audience. But was George really mad?

The king had been ill before, in 1765, but his illness had been hushed up. Its physical manifestations then seem to have been little more than a few pimples and oppression on the chest, although they were accompanied by mild depression and brief delirium. The illness in 1788 was much more severe and long-lasting and could not be kept from either Parliament or the public. The king's symptoms were meticulously recorded by his attendants. He suffered from abdominal pain of great severity. He was rheumatic. His body was covered with rashes and blisters. He had difficulty in getting his breath, and thus, not unsurprisingly, suffered from a rapid pulse, especially as his temperature rose above 103°F. These physical symptoms were accompanied by agitation, insomnia, confusion and delirium so that George was intermittently mentally incapacitated.

The doctors subjected the king to all the standard remedies of the time. His body was agonisingly blistered. Pints were drained from him in frequent orgies of blood-letting. Dr Willis, supremely confident, decided that the best way to calm down a patient thrashing about in pain and delirium was to confine him in a straitjacket. George, not unnaturally, objected violently. He roared in rage every time he saw Dr Willis approaching. When, in a more lucid moment, George had the temerity to complain of his treatment,

Dr Willis pointed out his great success in Bedlam and said the king had enjoyed the same treatment as that institution's inmates. George tartly replied that the difference was they did not have to pay £300 for the dubious pleasure of being confined in a straitjacket.

By late February 1789 George, as Willis had consistently promised, had fully recovered. The regency bill became unnecessary, Fox's hopes of becoming prime minister vanished and his list of his proposed cabinet remained in a drawer. But there was always a threat that George's illness would recur and as a result Pitt would not push the king too hard over Roman Catholic emancipation in 1801; even Fox, when he eventually became Prime Minister in 1807, was careful not to irritate George if it seemed that his illness might be returning.

It is, in fact, quite remarkable for someone with psychotic illness to have such long periods of normality broken by such short periods of mental disturbance. Yet for nearly 200 years no one queried the original diagnosis. Then in the 1960s medical researchers Ida Macalpine and Richard Hunter were struck by the similarity between George's physical symptoms, as reported at the time, and the signs of porphyria, a rare metabolic disease characterised by enzyme deficiency. The disease is named after the purple marble porphyry, and purple or purple-red is the usual colour of sufferers' urine during an acute attack. It was, of course, not possible for the researchers to examine samples of George's urine. They had to be content with cataloguing the king's symptoms as chronicled by his servants and doctors, and tracing porphyria through his present and past relatives. Porphyria is a very rare disease, yet it is present today in a number of German relatives of the British royal family and was probably suffered by James I, Henry VII's son Arthur, and possibly Charles I's brother Henry. Mary Queen of Scots' symptoms often resembled porphyria. They are not in themselves convincing because she was such a well-known hypochondriac, but perhaps not all her symptoms were feigned.

Then the researchers had some luck. They came across a letter from one of George's personal servants who referred to the port-wine stains in the king's chamber pot and how she had seen these stains on a previous occasion when he was ill. This clinched the diagnosis and it is now accepted that George was not mad. If he suffered from delirium, this was the result of the physical symptoms of porphyria, especially the fever, and his remarkable recoveries were due not to Dr Willis's straitjacket, but to the natural end of acute episodes of the disease. At first it was assumed that George's illness was intermittent porphyria, the more common form of the disease, but the discovery that George was sensitive to sunlight pins it down as the variegate form, a distinction of more interest to the medical profession than to historians.

In 1811 George began to sink into irreversible senile dementia. To his contemporaries this confirmed that his previous illnesses were bouts of madness, yet the two are not connected. George's porphyria made him prickly and unpredictable; his dementia deprived him of reality and sent him round the palace in his nightgown muttering 'Tom's a'cold'. The king's illness was not a mystery to his contemporaries: he suffered from bouts of madness. But in later years when madness became an unsatisfactory explanation for his other symptoms, the nature of his illness became a mystery, and it is only comparatively recently that this mystery has been satisfactorily explained. Those who still believe that George was mad are inheritors of the same misconception that deluded his contemporaries, and they have considerably less justification for their views.

THE MYSTERY OF THE ASSASSINATION OF AIREY NEAVE MP

The story of the murder of Airey Neave as he drove his car out of the House of Commons car park in 1979 made sensational headlines in the newspapers, not least on account of his closeness to Margaret Thatcher. But modern revelations have shown that the usual explanation offered for the bomb under his car was perhaps not the complete, or even the correct, one.

Neave enjoyed a dramatic career until the moment of his death. Born in 1916 into an old Norfolk family, he enjoyed the privileges of his upper-class background, entering Eton in 1929. In 1933, to brush up his German, he spent some time in Berlin, then under the rule of Adolf Hitler, where he experienced at first hand the impact of the Nazi regime on the German people. He went to Merton College, Oxford, in 1934 to study law, graduated with a third-class degree in 1938 and went up to London to read for the Bar. In the same year he joined the Territorial Army and was posted to an anti-aircraft searchlight regiment as a second lieutenant. There he underwent some training in time for the looming war. Posted to France in early 1940, he faced the invading columns of Guderian's Panzer divisions and took part in the desperate effort to halt their advance at Calais so as to facilitate the evacuation from Dunkirk. The British defences, however, were pulverised by the German advance, and Neave was wounded in action and captured. Confined in a prisoner-of-war camp near Kassel, he was later transferred to another, much less salubrious, one at Thorn on the Vistula. There he made his first rather disorganised attempt at escape. As the result of this he was again moved, this time to the high-security fortress of Colditz in Saxony.

It was from here that, after fifteen months, Neave made good his escape (at the second attempt) in early 1942 in the company of a Dutch officer who spoke better German than he did. In a series of hair-raising adventures the pair made their way by night-train across Germany to the Swiss border, and from there, after leaving his friend, Neave passed along what was known as the 'rat-line' through Vichy France and Spain to Gibraltar, whence he was returned to Britain by boat. He had already been contacted by MI9, a military intelligence group working to organise the return of escaped POWs to Britain, and it was not long before he found himself closely involved with the efforts of this branch of the secret service. He took control of the department at Room 900 at the War Office in September 1942 and for the remainder of the war spent a good deal of time rescuing almost 1,000 escapees. After the war he served, in a junior capacity, in the Nuremberg Trials of war criminals, where, though his knowledge of the law was slight (and in any case very rusty), he got to meet most of the surviving top brass of the Nazi movement. He also encountered the members of the Soviet panel of judges, whose obvious dread of, and subservience to, Stalin reinforced his already strong anti-Communist prejudices.

Returning to civvy street, and now having taken silk, Neave took up a career in politics. He was defeated at his first attempt to enter the House – for Thurrock (Essex) in the 1950 general election – and was again narrowly defeated after a recount of the votes for Ealing North in 1951. He soon transferred his attentions to the much safer seat of Abingdon in North Berkshire, which, on the retirement of the sitting member, he was elected to represent in a by-election in June 1953. This was his launch-pad to a career on the front bench. Unfortunately his rise was slow; it was not until 1959 that he became Under-Secretary of State for Air. Shortly after that he suffered a heart attack and was ordered by his doctors to rest.

Though he was returned to Parliament in 1959 with an increased majority of over 10,000 votes, he was denied appointment to office by Chief Whip Edward Heath, mainly, it must be said, on health grounds; but rancour was conceived between the two men – largely on the part of Neave, who bitterly resented his exclusion. As a result he played no more than a minor role in the final decline of the Tory government in the early 1960s, though he retained his seat at Abingdon in the election that brought Harold Wilson to power in 1964. With the fall of Alec Douglas Home in July 1965 he was an unenthusiastic witness to the choice of Edward Heath to head the shadow cabinet and entered perhaps the least effective of his political days.

Throughout this time, however, he maintained close links with a number of ex-POW welfare groups, with the Atomic Energy Research Establishment at Harwell, with the base at Aldermaston (scene of the notorious CND marches of the 1960s) – both close to or actually in his constituency – and with military intelligence, chiefly MI5 and MI6. He also began to take an interest in the affairs of Northern Ireland. His somewhat militaristic temperament led him to hate the Irish nationalists, the IRA and kindred paramilitary organisations. At the same time he continued to nurse his mistrust of Communist infiltration. He even saw the shadow of Communism in the militancy of British trade unions. He remained boyishly thrilled by cloak-and-dagger operations. Kevin Cahill, an Irish investigative reporter who knew him at the time, said of Neave that he was 'a conspirator's conspirator', adding that he was 'a deeply unpleasant and flawed man, and arrogant'.

The early 1970s were a time of mounting public dissatisfaction with the government and recurring economic and monetary crises for the country. Neave managed to retain his seat at Abingdon in both the February and October general elections in 1974, and, using his appointment to the 1922 Committee to strengthen his position in the party, began working to undermine Heath's already precarious authority. But it was to the relatively unknown figure of Margaret Thatcher that the rebels turned as their candidate for the leadership. He became her campaign manager in the run-up to the leadership election, and used all his skills of flattery, intrigue, undercover operations and misinformation to engineer her victory in early February 1975, thereby earning her undying gratitude and securing his own position as a power broker in the party. He was rewarded with the post of head of Thatcher's private office and Shadow Secretary of State for Northern Ireland – a minor and by tradition potentially troublesome post – when virtually any other shadow appointment was his for the asking.

In the twilight years before 1979, when Thatcher eventually came to power, he strengthened his links with MI5, entrenched his position against the threat of Communism, militant trade unionism and Irish subversion, and helped to found a new and potentially far-reaching movement, the National Association for Freedom (NAFF), which was strongly linked to influential bodies of British industrialists. Further, though nothing was known of it at the time – it was later revealed by a dissident intelligence officer called Peter Wright in his book *Spycatcher*, which the government did its best to suppress – Neave was connected with a group called Tory Action which planned to undermine and even to overthrow the Wilson government and to sketch in the outlines of right-wing organisations that would assume political power in its place. In 1987 Ken Livingstone, Labour MP for Brent East, tried in the House of Commons to expose this conspiracy, but he was howled down by right-wingers and his views denounced as 'deeply offensive'. Some of Neave's associates came to believe that he was moving imperceptibly from being an opponent of left-wing agitation and infiltration to becoming a supporter of right-wing infiltration.

Meantime, his interest in the Ulster problem con-tinued to grow. He became an expert in the subject, often working as closely as his political allegiances would permit first with Mervyn Rees and later with

Roy Mason during their stints for the Labour government as Northern Ireland secretary. He was a strong supporter of internment, opposed the importation of arms into Ulster, especially from the Soviet bloc, and became an adherent of Operation Clockwork Orange, a scheme to undermine terrorists in Northern Ireland through the use of press misinformation. He came in the end to support a policy of repudiating devolution, and even power-sharing, by aiming to reintegrate Northern Ireland with mainland Britain. This objective, however, distanced his position from that of the USA, which preferred to encourage closer links with the Irish Republic as a means of resolving the problem – a solution that was anathema to Neave. That by this time he had become a dangerously loose cannon is indicated by two further pointers: he strongly supported what was known at the time as the shoot-to-kill policy in dealing with protesters; and he is said – even more bizarrely – to have toyed with the idea, if Callaghan resigned, of having Tony Benn assassinated (if he became the new Labour leader) to prevent him taking office.

In late March 1979 the Callaghan government was defeated by a single vote in the House and the prime minister resigned, calling a general election for 3 May. A seat at the cabinet table was about to beckon for Airey Neave. However, the country was denied the experience of having him as Northern Ireland secretary. The Irish National Liberation Army (INLA) – which had returned the youthful Bernadette Devlin to Parliament in 1969 – was already planning to assassinate Neave. Its volunteers travelled to London for the job. They knew his address in Westminster Gardens; they were familiar with his blue Vauxhall and its registration number. Shortly before 3 p.m. on

30 March, as Neave was driving up the ramp from the car park into Westminster Yard, a bomb exploded under his car in the confined space of the steep exit, blowing out its doors, windows and bonnet, and punching up the roof. Neave died in hospital an hour later. The INLA claimed credit for the killing.

Margaret Thatcher was utterly shattered by the murder and said of him immediately afterwards, 'Airey was a very gentle and unassuming man, but absolutely tenacious in pursuit of everything he believed in, and strong to root out injustice.' This was a view that was widely shared. Security arrangements in the precincts of the Palace of Westminster were abruptly tightened in case the bomb had been placed under the car there and not while it was parked at the MP's home; but all this seemed like shutting the stable door after the horse had gone.

There were some peculiar features to the case. For one thing, the INLA had a very limited membership, less than 200, to undertake such an ambitious operation; and, for another, it contained so many moles that MI5 knew almost as much about its activities as its own leadership did. Also, the explosive used was very specialised (it looked rather like pink soap), and the technology of the actual bomb (it was a mercury-tilt device that went off when the vehicle was on a slope and the mercury ran along a tube to complete an electrical circuit) was supposedly beyond the capability of the INLA. Police enquiries were laborious and protracted, sometimes rather impeded by lively media interest both from the press and the TV, but ultimately quite fruitless.

The inquest into Neave's death was delayed until October for the police to make enquiries, but though numerous people were pulled in for questioning, there was no evidence against any of them and all were released without charge. In the meantime, under cover of security, the SAS (Special Air Service, the elite of paramilitary shock troops) and the UDA (the Ulster Defence Association), working in close collaboration in Operation Ranc, wrought a terrible revenge on the INLA, murdering much of its leadership and driving its members into hiding. There was even an attack on the life of Bernadette Devlin (now Bernadette McAliskey) when the UDA broke down the door of her house near Coalisland and shot her eight times.

Neave's connection with the secret services continued to be systematically covered up, even from those conducting the inquiry. It was Enoch Powell, the maverick Tory MP now in the Ulster Unionist camp, who blew the gaff on all this skulduggery and put forward a startling new version of the story. He linked Neave's murder with a number of earlier killings, including the deaths of Lord Mountbatten and of Robert Bradford, the Unionist politician, suggesting that two branches of the 'secret state' were in conflict with each other. He believed these intrigues were part of an organised attempt already begun to bring together the US, the UK and the Irish Republic in a deal to negotiate an Irish settlement that would eliminate Stormont, a deal to which Neave was a major obstacle. Powell pointed out, in his usual Delphic manner, similarities between this case and CIA interference in Iran and Central America, and seemed to suggest that Neave's death was the result of CIA intrigue. His surprise statement reinforced the view already put forward that mercury-tilt technology was typically part of the CIA's armoury.

Powell was not alone in his opinion that there was conflict between different branches of military intelligence. Gerald James, former head of an ordnance firm called Astra Holdings, confirmed the Wright opinion that Neave had been deeply involved in operations to prepare for 'civil breakdown' in the 1970s, but James went on to declare that Neave's efforts to sort out and clean up the intelligence and security services incurred their hostility; and, because he was seen as a danger to the 'secret state', they decided to eliminate him.

It must be said that there are many, including members of Neave's own family, who reject all these allegations as outrageous and unfounded. These people suggested that Neave was one of the old-style Conservatives, with all their 'dignity and manners and all their intellectual limitations'. They question the validity of the evidence produced against him, insisting that nearly all was gossip put about by his opponents.

So who killed Airey Neave and for what reason? Perhaps the explanation put forward in 2001 by surviving members of the INLA was the true one: that the murder was carried out by 'sleepers', i.e. people sympathetic to the Irish cause but without any earlier connection with terrorism and with no criminal record, whose identity was never divulged to others and of whom there were no records kept, even in the INLA's most secret files. These people carried out what was to them an execution, after which they played no further part in the movement. They were never detected because they were 'clean' and at present are presumably still living in the Irish Republic, safe from detection.

5

Military, Naval and Air Mysteries

WHAT SANK THE *MARY ROSE*?

In the summer of 1545 the Mary Rose, *the veteran flagship of Henry VIII's fleet, sailed into action against the French in the Solent. England faced international condemnation as the result from Henry's Reformation of the Church, and Francis I exploited this by sending a large force of up to 200 warships and fighting galleys equipped with about ninety heavy cannon and hundreds of soldiers and archers in an expedition against Portsmouth. Henry himself watched apprehensively from the shore as his minuscule fleet of about thirty ships, still awaiting the arrival of the score or more of hired vessels engaged by the king for the purpose, put out against the enemy behind his flagship, the* Mary Rose. *Taking the familiar south-west channel in the direction of the shoreline of the Isle of Wight and the French fleet, the* Mary Rose *discharged her port broadside and then put about to discharge her starboard guns. Instead she heeled over as she turned, capsized and sank in the full view of the horrified spectators, leaving only about twenty-five survivors clinging to the superstructure. In a single inexplicable moment were lost the pride of England's navy and over 400 soldiers and sailors. How did the catastrophe happen, and what caused it?*

This was a splendid wooden ship, the pride of the navy and believed by the experts to be virtually unsinkable. How could it be so finally and so catastrophically lost? The mystery remains unsolved to this day, though after 500 years recent studies by marine engineers and historical researchers have pointed the way to a number of reasonable explanations.

In 1982 an expedition of marine archaeologists salvaged what remained of the *Mary Rose*. Only the starboard side of the vessel, long silted up in the soft mud of the Solent, had survived. The expedition's members recovered as much as they could of the wreck, chemically preserved it and undertook its display in what was essentially a specially prepared damp cellar in Portsmouth. The ship and the documentary material relating to her were then made the subject of a detailed inquiry whose results were not complete until 1999. The possible causes of the disaster may be summarised as follows:

(1) The *Mary Rose* was sunk by a single hit, or a number of hits, from the French fleet. Such a lucky shot might technically have been possible if it had come from one of the heavy brass cannon in the bows of the attacking galleys. Unlike other contemporary cannon, which fired iron shot smaller than a human fist, the cannon aboard the galleys delivered heavy stone shots of about 4 kilogrammes mass and these could do considerable damage where they struck. The fact that no evidence survives of such an impact in the wreck is not conclusive, since any shot would have struck the port side of the vessel, all of which has now disappeared. However, there is no contemporary

evidence of a sixteenth-century warship being sunk by gunfire only. Furthermore, the walls and bulkheads of the *Mary Rose* were 35 centimetres thick, and it seems unlikely that gunfire alone could have been the cause of her sudden loss.

(2) The *Mary Rose* had become critically unstable as the result of the recent refit ordered by the king. The ship was in fact over thirty years old and had already fought successfully against the French in a naval battle in 1512. The king now wished to update her in the interests of personal and national prestige, and to introduce the very latest onboard technological improvements. In particular he wished to instal eight of the newly available long-range brass cannon, four on the port side and four on the starboard, to supplement the considerable armament the ship already carried. Each of these cannon weighed a tonne and their supporting carriage a further 200 kilogrammes. Any rebuilding would have necessitated new timbers, further adding to the weight. Dendrochronologists found that the new timbers installed in the vessel were cut from trees felled in 1542 and thus probably installed at the time of the refit. The new armament had to be placed low down so that the vessel did not become top heavy, and shuttered gun-ports fitted so that the sea would not get in as the ship turned. But the effect of all these modifications, whatever their prestige value, would have been to render the *Mary Rose* less seaworthy than she had been previously.

(3) The refitted *Mary Rose* was commanded by newly appointed and relatively inexperienced officers.

The king, ashore in Southsea Castle in the company of the wife of Sir George Carew, who had been selected as Vice-Admiral and Commander only days before, was merely following the traditional custom in choosing gentlemen as senior officers, leaving the actual management of the ship in the hands of the master and his crew. Carew might have suggested (and by the look of his correspondence did suggest) that any shortcoming in the ship's performance was due to their drunkenness and insubordination. It is much more likely that it was the result of the amateurism and incompetence of the ship's officers. Could it be that, in the confusion and panic of battle, they had issued contradictory orders overriding the instructions of the professional master – or perhaps prevented the issue of any orders at all?

(4) The *Mary Rose* may also have been dangerously overloaded at the time she went into action. She was supposed to have a complement of 415 men, composed of 200 mariners, 30 gunners and 185 soldiers ready for transfer to any French vessel that was to be boarded during the action. The soldiers were to be quartered in the two castles, fore and aft at the two highest portions of the ship. To make the boarding of the *Mary Rose* herself more difficult, the level areas of the main deck between the two castles were covered with stout rope netting. This had the effect not only of impeding foreigners while they boarded the ship, but simultaneously preventing anyone below decks in the *Mary Rose* from making their escape if they needed.

It seems likely, however, that the official figure of
185 seriously underestimated the number of
soldiers in the two castles. Contemporary records
suggest that there were over 400 soldiers aboard.
The officers would naturally want as many soldiers
as possible available in case of boarding, and the
established custom, as seen in the case of other
vessels involved in similar actions, was to take on a
total complement equivalent to 75 per cent of the
tonnage of the ship – in the case of the *Mary Rose*,
a ship of 800 tonnes, 600 men altogether. Since
every soldier, together with his equipment, would
weigh about 100 kilogrammes, the addition of an
extra 200 soldiers would make the ship top heavier
by about 20 tonnes, all perched in the castles fore
and aft. Professional seamen might have been
aware of the dangers of such an undertaking, but
gentlemen amateurs perhaps not.

(5) Contemporary eye-witness accounts suggested that
the *Mary Rose* sank during the manoeuvre of
putting about, and the sinking may have been due
to the angle of the ship during the turn. With the
vessel's extra load and the installation of the new
gun-ports just above the waterline, her angle during
the turning manoeuvre may have been sufficient to
permit the taking aboard of a good deal of seawater,
particularly if the ports had been left open. Unlikely as such an omission may seem for an
experienced crew, the fact remains that there had
been few, if any, regular sea-trials for the refitted
ship, and this manoeuvre took place at a time of
panic and confusion because of the battle. Furthermore, at the time of salvage these ports were all

found open. A cubic metre of water weighs a tonne and the shipping of tonnes of water undoubtedly would have further diminished the seaworthiness of the vessel. Eye-witnesses also suggested that the ship was overtaken by a sudden squall, and this might well have tipped the *Mary Rose* further over, away from the wind.

Though the reason for the sinking remains a mystery, in the eyes of the experts the most likely explanation would seem to lie in an unfortunate combination of circumstances: the overenthusiastic refitting of an old warship, inadequacies in its crewing and command, its serious overloading with men and armaments, and a dangerous manoeuvre perhaps in squally conditions with open gun-ports close to the waterline. But this is no more than a well-informed guess nearly five centuries after the event. The precise explanation for the catastrophe may never be known.

THE INEXPLICABLE MYSTERY OF THE
MARY CELESTE

The fate of the Mary Celeste *on a voyage from New York to Europe in 1872 was so bizarre that the whole story rates as one of the most impenetrable of maritime legends, for which a whole variety of different explanations has been offered.*

It was in 1867 that four Americans bought the ship. She had a bad reputation and was widely thought to be unlucky. Over the next five years her new owners used her to carry cargoes between Britain, the USA and the

Mediterranean. On 5 November 1872 the *Mary Celeste* left New York carrying 1,700 barrels of industrial alcohol, a crew of eight and two passengers, the wife and two-year-old daughter of Captain Benjamin Briggs. Four weeks later the *Dei Gratia*, commanded by Captain David Morehouse, sighted the *Mary Celeste* about 200 miles north-west of the Azores. He observed that the ship's wheel was unmanned and unsecured. On 5 December he boarded and discovered that the vessel was deserted, her whole crew missing. There was no evidence of violence aboard or of boarding, and the ship's cargo was intact. The ship's cat was asleep on a locker in the mess room and there was an untouched meal set out on the table, with three cups of tea untouched. The lifeboats were still secured in their normal places on the superstructure, but the yawl, normally towed behind the vessel, had been cut loose and was missing, as was a quantity of navigational equipment. Why should ten people leave a perfectly seaworthy ship that carried enough food to last them for six months and put off in a small open boat?

Various hypotheses put forward to explain the mystery are so utterly unlikely as to be capable of being discarded at once. That the problem was brought about by an attack by beings from outer space bears no serious consideration. That the tragedy occurred because of the malign forces of the Bermuda Triangle is spoiled chiefly by the fact that the event took place 200 miles east of the Azores and well outside its baleful influence. That the crew were picked off one by one by a giant octopus which ate them was the theory put forward in 1923 by L. du Garde Peach, but this, too, seems beyond the bounds of reasonable likelihood. Earlier, Conan Doyle in one of his short stories* had put forward the almost equally unlikely theory that the crew had been made up by crimps (on-shore agents who supplied pressed men to ships short of crew) in New York who had sent aboard a gang of Negroes and these men had taken it into their heads to murder everybody else aboard and then make a settlement on an island nearby – a theory whose sole merit appeared to be that it explained the missing yawl boat and the navigational equipment, though it did not explain why the names of these additional men were not on the crew list. However, leaving such improbabilities as these aside, there seem to be six reasonably plausible explanations for the disaster.

Raids by Riff pirates from nearby islands or from North Africa. The Court of Inquiry at Gibraltar into the salvage claim put forward by the master of the *Dei Gratia* later considered this possibility but discarded it.** Pirate raids were not unknown in these seas, but

---

* It was he who first mentioned the ship's cat and the uneaten meal in the mess room, and this detail may have been his invention to add verisimilitude to his story. This story was one of his first successes and was published in *Cornhill Magazine* in 1833 under the title of *J. Habakuk Jephson's Statement*. A Court of Inquiry held in Gibraltar, where the chief counsel resisting the salvage claim minutely probed all the relevant facts, did not refer to such details as these.

** This was in spite of a very probing performance from the chief counsel resisting the master of the *Dei Gratia*'s salvage claim. The counsel somehow got it into his head that the claim was bogus and questioned the salvage team minutely about all the details. He finally got the salvage award substantially reduced.

the evidence of those who examined the vessel both at the time of the boarding and subsequently when it reached land had been unanimously in agreement that there was no sign of a struggle. There were oddly unexplained marks on the prow suggesting that it had perhaps been in a collision, though no mention of any such accident appeared in the ship's log. Furthermore, two sails were torn, though the ship was still making progress using two others that remained rigged. The rest of the masts were bare.

Mutiny. There seemed to be no obvious reason for a mutiny, though it was suggested that there may have been men aboard (possibly supplied by New York crimps) in addition to the seven named on the crew list, three of whom were American and the other four Germans from East Prussia. But where were the mutineers? There were later stories about a skeleton being found on the island of St Paul not too far away, and even of a message in a bottle written in German, but no hard evidence for any of this was ever forthcoming.

Fire and explosion. The ship had left New York in freezing weather, but it was well known that a cargo of alcohol had to be prudently treated on voyage. If it got warm it could give off fumes that were explosive. It was suggested that such an explosion took place, followed by a fire in which those on board had taken to the yawl to save themselves (thus explaining why it was missing). However, the hatch of the hold in which the alcohol was stored was off. Whether this was because the force of the explosion had blown it off, or whether it had been properly left off to allow the fumes to escape, no one sought to question. In any case there was no sign

167

of fire and the cargo was intact. This also gave the lie to the suggestion that crew members had broached the cargo and that the affair was the result of a drunken brawl (since the cargo was of industrial alcohol, it was not fit for drinking).

The explosion theory was supported by a TV transmission (*The Mystery of the Mary Celeste*) in May 2006, which described scientific experiments in which such explosions were simulated and which left no traces of fire afterwards. But, granted that such an unlikely scenario was possible, this ingenious theory did not explain why the captain and crew did not go back on board after a day or so (or even after an hour), just as soon as they realised that their ship was not going to explode.

Murder and suicide. By conviction Captain Briggs was a total abstainer, but he was known to be a rather heavy-handed man, occasionally given to bouts of religious mania, and it was suggested that perhaps in a fit of madness he killed his wife and daughter and then went on to murder the whole crew. When he recovered his wits it was proposed he might have thrown himself overboard. Again, absence of a struggle told against this explanation. Interest in this story increased when it was alleged that a sword had been found aboard with a crusted blade and that there were dark spots on the deck planking; but when a forensic examination of the weapon took place at Gibraltar, the suspected substance turned out to be citrate of iron.*

---

* Hostile counsel derided the leader of the boarding party's claim that he thought the marks on the blade were rust, but found it difficult to gainsay the fact that there was no evidence of bloodstains.

Accident. Another explanation for the affair surfaced in 1913 when an account of a bizarre diving accident was published in the *Strand* magazine. One Abel Fosdyke claimed to have travelled on the vessel as a secret passenger. He said that he had witnessed what had taken place. (He certainly was 'secret'; no one had heard of him before.) He claimed that the captain had had a special structure built at the bows from which passengers could dive and swim, and which could also be used as an observation platform. On the day in question one of the swimmers let out an agonising yell; everyone else crowded onto this structure for a better look, whereupon it collapsed under their weight and plunged them into the sea. All were lost except Fosdyke, who clung to the wreckage and eventually was washed ashore on the North African coast. Fosdyke was an educated man and his employer found notes on the disaster among his effects. He published them in the *Strand* magazine, believing there was no reason why Fosdyke should have made up such a story. The account helped to explain the peculiar marks on the prow of the ship, where the superstructure could have been slotted in; but it left many unanswered questions. Chiefly there was no corroboration of the account; further, there was no explanation of why anyone should wish to swim from a vessel proceeding at several knots, especially in shark-infested waters. In any event, Fosdyke's version of the details of the ship and its crew was wildly inaccurate. The likelihood remains that the whole story was fictitious.

Conspiracy. It seemed odd that the abandoned ship had been found by Captain Morehouse of the

Dei Gratia, a vessel that had put out from New York exactly a week before the *Mary Celeste* on a similar course and bound for the same destination. This extraordinary coincidence was complicated by the fact that Briggs and Morehouse were in fact friends. Suspicion grew that the salvage claim was an insurance fraud. The *Mary Celeste* had been insured by the Mutual Insurance Company of New York for $14,000, and the cargo had also been insured at Lloyd's for £6,500 (at an exchange rate of $5 to the pound this was a much bigger sum). It was said that perhaps Morehouse intended to claim a large sum for salvaging the *Mary Celeste*, and that he hoped to share what would have seemed a substantial fortune to two poor seamen, especially if their business was not going well. The counsel resisting the salvage claim seems to have suspected something like this and was successful in persuading the Court of Inquiry to award a derisory sum of less than £2,000 instead of the full claim. Such a conspiracy seems to some to be the most likely explanation for the mystery. But, even if the fraud theory was true, the ruse was unsuccessful: Captain Briggs and his family were never seen or heard of again, and Captain Morehouse failed to secure the full salvage money for recovering the ship.

So the *Mary Celeste* affair must remain a baffling and an unsolved mystery. No fewer than eight stories or novels have been written on the subject, and the tale continues to fascinate those who study it. This mystery shows how, in the days before the techniques of criminal evidence were as rigorous as they are at present, fanciful stories could grow up to obscure the truth of what really happened.

The story of the *Mary Celeste* ends rather prosaically. In 2001 her wreck was discovered by divers off the coast of Haiti. After the 1872 episode the ship changed hands numerous times, being sold over and over again before genuinely being scuttled as part of an insurance fraud in 1885. When he claimed the insurance her captain claimed she was carrying valuable cargo. In fact, the ship was laden with boots and cat food.

WHAT SANK THE *TITANIC*?

Just before midnight on 14 April 1912 the liner Titanic *struck an iceberg. In less than two and a half hours the ship sank. For most of the twentieth century there was no mystery attached to this disaster; unchallenged explanations were offered for all the questions that might be asked. Captain Smith was foolhardy. The ship was going too fast. She had insufficient lifeboats. She had ignored iceberg warnings from other vessels. The casualties would have been fewer if the first boats to be launched had not been half empty. The sinking would not have occurred if only two or even three watertight compartments had been pierced by the iceberg, but the 300-foot gash would have been too much for any vessel. The ship's band was not playing 'Nearer My God to Thee' as she sank. The nearest vessel to the* Titanic, *the* Californian, *would have arrived much earlier had its radio not been switched off. These and other issues were dealt with by the enquiries held soon after the disaster on both sides of the Atlantic. But they did not have the benefit of the discovery of the wreck on the ocean floor – this was*

*made in 1985. If they had, the explanation of why
the ship sank so rapidly, or indeed why it sank at
all, would have needed drastic revision.*

Once the ship's resting place at the bottom of the ocean
was discovered, new technology was used to check the
extent of the initial iceberg damage. Sub-bottom
profilers, which work electronically to transmit and
receive low-frequency acoustic signals, were able to
create digital images of the wreck. It was found that
there was no 300-foot gash. Instead the damage consisted of a series of six thin slits, some of them no more
than an inch wide. The total area of damage was 'no
more than 12 square feet – about the size of a human
body'. It seemed that the slits mostly ran along the lines
where the hull plates had been riveted together. These
plates were, according to the original specifications,
made of Siemens-Martin formula steel – the best
available at that time, of battleship quality, and strongly
resistant to corrosion. Since the White Star line had
paid for the *Titanic* on a cost basis with profit added as a
percentage, there was no reason for any contractor to
substitute lower quality steel to save on the bill. Yet
steel recovered from the hull in later operations was
found to contain a large proportion of silicate slag. This
impurity is intrinsic in wrought iron but in steel it is
undesirable because it makes the metal brittle. This
brittleness may have contributed to plate fracture in the
Titanic because on the day of the sinking there was a
rapid fall in water temperature from +6°C to −2°C, a
temperature at which brittle fracture is much more
likely to occur.

An even more important discovery was made when
examples of the *Titanic*'s rivets were brought to the

surface. These rivets, of which there were over 3 million, were mainly used to hold the plates together, and in some parts were tripled or even quadrupled for greater strength. Welding was not yet common practice in shipbuilding, and the rivets were inserted either by hand or, as in the *Titanic*, hydraulically. In either case they had to be reasonably malleable, because once they had been pushed through the holes in the hull plates the ends had to be squeezed into a rounded head so that they could lock the plates rigidly together. Of the few rivets so far brought up and examined, almost half are contaminated with slag, which would have weakened them and made them less likely to withstand the impact of the iceberg. With the initial crash the plates would have rippled and the rivet heads would have sheared. There would have been leakage rather than massive flooding, and this is what took place in the forward compartments.

When the design engineers said that the ship was 'practically unsinkable' they only anticipated a collision with another vessel, either forward at the bows or at right angles against the hull. Such a collision would not be expected to penetrate more than two of the fifteen watertight compartments at any one time; the compartment doors would be shut electrically from the bridge, and the ship would be safe. But the compartments were not absolutely watertight. If the water tipped over the bulkheads, general flooding would occur, and in some compartments the bulkheads were only 2½ feet above the water line. The long lateral scraping collision with an iceberg was not allowed for in the designs. It separated the plates in five compartments, if only by a matter of inches. At this point nothing could stop the water surging in. As the plates separated, enormous pressure of sea water would have prevented them being closed again. And as the forward compartments filled, the ship tilted forwards and water ran back over the bulkheads of the other compartments.

Some confirmation of this general theory is to be found in damage caused to the *Titanic*'s sister ship, the *Olympic*. When she was involved in a collision in 1911 rivet heads popped off, releasing the plates, and photographs show vacant holes where the rivets should have been. Similar holes without rivets have been observed on parts of the *Titanic*'s hull. The brittleness of the hull plates would have contributed to the rippling, but this weakness varied from compartment to compartment and from plate to plate. It seems likely that both plate brittleness and rivet weakness made a major contribution to the damage caused by the iceberg, but in what proportion and to what extent remains the object of further study and enquiry. Certainly the traditional view of the sinking is a misconception which requires considerable modification.

THE MYSTERY OF THE SINKING OF THE *LUSITANIA*

The torpedoing of the Lusitania *was one of the many 'evil deeds' attributed to the Germans in the First World War. It caused outrage in the USA, where it aroused much anti-German feeling and damaged the German cause. On the one hand, the British claimed that the* Lusitania *was an unarmed passenger ship which was not carrying contraband of war; and that her sinking without warning by a U-boat was an unpardonable atrocity. On the other, the Germans claimed that the ship was secretly transporting explosives and ammunition from a neutral USA to Britain, putting civilians at risk and brazenly violating international law; and that she had been specifically targeted because of the contraband she was carrying. The British claim was a downright lie; the German one was misleading. Is it now possible to unravel the true facts of the sinking from the mass of legend and propaganda enveloping it?*

The First World War had broken out over most of Europe by early August 1914. Although the majority, though by no means all, of its citizens sympathised with Britain and France, the USA was determined to maintain a benevolent neutrality. But this was difficult to do while the British navy was attempting to blockade Germany, and while German submarines were sinking merchant vessels en route for Britain. At first German submarines observed the Cruiser rules, which meant they surfaced and gave a merchant ship's crew time to take to the lifeboats before sinking their vessel. But when the British Admiralty authorised merchant ships to carry guns and disguised naval vessels as merchant ones (Q-boats), the Germans began to suffer U-boat losses. Cautious U-boat captains adopted the policy of 'when in doubt sink on sight', and they made no exceptions for passenger ships. This policy was given official German backing in 1915. It seemed inevitable that American citizens on British ships would be at risk.

All the same, the *Lusitania* was thought to be safe. She was the finest ship in the Cunard line. With four great funnels towering 75 feet over the boat deck, the liner was 780 feet long, had a displacement of 32,500 tons and could reach a maximum speed of 26 knots,

easily surpassing any other ship afloat. Her first-class
accommodation was the height of luxury with a gilt-
and-white domed dining room, a drawing room
panelled in mahogany, a smoking room and libraries,
and a 24-bed hospital. Her master, Captain William
Turner, was immensely proud of his ship. When the
Germans published in New York a notice to intending
passengers warning them that they were in a war zone
and were travelling at their own risk, he laughed it off.
'The best joke I've heard in many days,' he said, 'this
talk of torpedoing the *Lusitania*!'

On 1 May 1915 the passengers, most of them British,
set sail from New York for Liverpool and were expected
in Europe in little more than seven days. But on 7 May,
off the Old Head of Kinsale on the southern coast of
Ireland, they had an unexpected encounter with the
German submarine *U-20*. Its master, Kapitänleutnant
Walther Schwieger, had been at sea since late April,
and only the previous day had sunk two ships,
allowing the crew to abandon one but sinking the other
without warning. He had only two torpedoes left. He
sighted the *Lusitania* on the horizon in the early
afternoon, steaming a perfectly straight course at a
steady speed in order to get an exact fix on the head-
land. Approaching cautiously, he fired his first torpedo
from periscope depth at a range of 700 metres. He saw
the explosion and its results. Satisfied that the ship was
rapidly foundering, he decided against firing his
second torpedo, downed periscope and headed for
home, leaving the *Lusitania* to her fate.

Within seconds the *Lusitania* was listing 15 degrees
to starboard. The passengers erupted onto the deck and
scrambled madly for the boats. As the bow went under
there was panic. Some tried to launch the lifeboats on

their own, but the ship was still moving quite fast and the lifeboats capsized; others stripped to their underwear and simply jumped into the sea. A total of 1,201 persons were drowned, including 785 passengers and 413 crew. In addition there were three stowaways whose identities were never established, and several of the bodies washed ashore remained unidentified. The ship sank in 18 minutes. Other vessels of a similar size had been much slower to founder: the *Titanic*, for example, had taken less than two and a half hours to go down in 1912.

The reason for the catastrophic speed of the sinking was said to have been a second, much bigger, explosion which ripped the ship apart. At the initial inquest on the sinking of the ship, under Lord Mersey, the Admiralty explained the second explosion by claiming that the U-boat had fired two torpedoes. That allegation was easily disproved. For one thing, the German Ministry of the Marine had evidence against it; for another, there was ample testimony from survivors that the second explosion had originated within the ship itself.

The second blast may have been an engine-room explosion. It could have been caused by one or more of a number of things. The captain had been instructed to take six of the boilers of the *Lusitania* out of commission to save on coal and labour; this not only had the effect of reducing the liner's speed from 26 knots to 21, but it also meant that the remaining boilers were working much harder than usual. There may have been a boiler explosion, or one in the steamline* where

---

* The line of piping leading the pressurised steam from the boilers to the ship's engines.

the rush of cold water could have produced a catastrophic reduction in pressure; or, there may have been
an explosion in the engine room itself if damp, warm
air laden with coal dust combusted after the torpedo
hit. None of these explanations seems likely. For one
thing, it is almost impossible to obtain a suitable mix
of coal dust and damp air to make such an explosion,
even in carefully controlled laboratory conditions; for
another, there were survivors from the engine rooms
who testified that no such explosion took place.

Yet another explanation is to hand. Whether or not it
is acceptable depends on whether the cock-up or the
conspiracy theory of history is preferred. Was the
captain to blame, or did the Admiralty frame him?
There is no doubt that the Admiralty issued what
appear to be contradictory orders: they required
Captain Turner to proceed at full speed, yet they also
instructed him to deactivate six of his boilers, which
had the effect of cutting his speed to 21 knots, and, as
he passed the Old Head of Kinsale, to 18 knots. There
is also a mysterious gap lasting for several hours in the
records of communications between the *Lusitania* and
the Admiralty, which to some suggests a cover-up of
what really happened. This version of events helps
further to explain the Admiralty's willingness to put
the blame on Captain Turner personally.

Undoubtedly the most likely explanation for the
second explosion (and the most damaging of all) arises
from the munitions that the ship was believed to be
carrying. Both the commissions of inquiry into the
sinking, the British one in June 1915 and the American
one in the summer of 1918, agreed in their conclusion
that the *Lusitania* was not carrying war contraband.
Both were wrong. Several copies of the cargo manifest

show that the *Lusitania* had ammunition aboard. There were 4,200 cases of rifle bullets (1,000 bullets per case), 1,250 cases of shrapnel shells (unfilled) and 18 cases of percussion fuses; all these were rather misleadingly labelled 'Non-Explosive in Bulk' and hence were allowed under the rules of war. The manifests were incomplete, however, and the contents of two of the cargo holds have never been revealed. It seems likely that they contained quantities of gun cotton – a highly explosive material produced by impregnating cotton fibre with nitric and sulphuric acid – possibly hidden in a consignment of furs. The German authorities in New York certainly suspected that the ship was carrying cargo which was forbidden by American law and should never have been transported on a passenger liner, but it is unlikely that they had any specific proof. The press warnings from the German consulate in New York against travelling on the liner did not, however, mention contraband. The German argument about contraband came after the sinking; the commander of *U-20* did not even know until the last minute which ship he was torpedoing, let alone what the vessel was carrying. He had sunk the *Lusitania* on sight, and the German defence that the ship was a legitimate war target on account of its cargo was shaky to say the least.

The subsequent action of the British Admiralty in trying to destroy Turner's reputation makes sense only if it was trying to undermine the captain's credibility in case of any revealing disclosures he might make later. Any other revelations were circumvented by the fortuitously incomplete state of the manifests. This dark suspicion is reinforced by the astonishing remark of Winston Churchill, First Sea Lord, to Walter Runciman, President of the Board of Trade, in 1915. He said, 'It is important to attract neutral shipping to our shores in the hope of embroiling the United States with Germany.' Such a statement chimes in with the idea that the Admiralty connived in a plot to risk the lives of women and children in placing them aboard a ship illegally loaded with arms and explosives, and this makes the conspiracy theory look more likely. Therefore the families of the bereaved, as well as the Germans, may have had real cause to feel aggrieved. The British were not as innocent as they pretended, and the German less guilty than was originally alleged.

So it seems possible to suggest the truth behind this mystery. In this context it is worth noting that a US salvage concern, Kinvarra Shipping, has bought the wreck and planned in 2003 to salvage what it could, partly in the interests of history and partly for the sale of whatever material could be recovered. The organisers, however, have so far met with the unyielding opposition of the government of the Irish Republic, which has in recent years extended its territorial waters from 3 miles to 12 and now claims proprietorship of the wreck. Whether the salvage goes ahead depends on the outcome of a legal case which the salvage company is at present bringing against the Republic.

WHAT CAUSED THE *HINDENBURG* DISASTER?

The disaster that struck the German dirigible Hindenburg *in 1937 is generally attributed to the highly dangerous properties of hydrogen as a lifting agent. This verdict, however, was based on hasty or defective research; more recent enquiries have suggested a quite different cause.*

The *Hindenburg* was a 245-metre airship of conventional Zeppelin design built and launched by the Zeppelin Company at Friedrichshafen, Germany, in 1936. It had a maximum speed of 84mph and a cruising speed of 78mph; it could carry upwards of 100 passengers and a considerable amount of commercial freight. During 1936 the vessel inaugurated commercial air services across the North Atlantic by carrying over 1,000 passengers and substantial cargoes between Germany and the United States on ten scheduled flights. It also made a number of other voyages to other destinations in the New World. Hitler was very proud of the vessel and wished it to be known as the *Adolf Hitler*, a request its owners politely refused.

On 6 May 1937, while landing at Lakehurst, New Jersey, the hydrogen-filled *Hindenburg* suddenly burst into flames, fell to the ground and was completely destroyed. Thirty-six of the ninety-seven persons aboard were killed and a larger number injured. Since the weather at the time was stormy and the airship had been delayed in landing by the need to manoeuvre between two nearby thunderstorms, the fire was generally attributed to the discharge of atmospheric electricity, or static, in the vicinity of hydrogen gas which was being vented from the airship. The accident caused a sensation throughout the world, and prompted the setting up of a commission of inquiry by the US Department of Commerce. This inquiry spent some time investigating the crash. The Zeppelin Company, whose prestige was put at risk by the disaster, established a similar inquiry of its own, though the results were never published.

Theories explaining the incident abounded. They revolved round the mystery of how the hydrogen enclosed in the lifting bags of the *Hindenburg* could have been ignited. Suspicion fell at first on a German citizen, a professional acrobat, who was suspected of climbing up between the bags inside the shell with a view to taking photographs with a flash camera, so accidentally triggering the explosion that led to the fire. But such an explanation seemed doubtful and it was not long before the hypothesis was discarded. There was speculation, too, about the possibility of sabotage carried out by anti-Nazi fanatics seeking to discredit the Third Reich. Though this was closely examined, no proof of the suggestion was ever produced. In the end, the investigators felt obliged to put the blame on the highly inflammable nature of hydrogen, concluding that it was too dangerous to be used in such quantities for purposes of transportation. The *Hindenburg* disaster marked the end of hydrogen-filled rigid airships in commercial air transport. Though there was one already nearly finished in Germany, further research and development were abandoned and with the outbreak of war in 1939 no more was heard of airship transportation.

However, in the 1990s NASA rocket scientists remained dissatisfied with the verdict on the disaster. They were convinced that hydrogen, far from being dangerous, was one of the best and most environmentally friendly forms of fuel. Whether used as a lifting agent or burned as fuel, when combined with oxygen it produces as a residue nothing more harmful than steam. They believed that in spite of all the time and energy spent on the *Hindenburg* investigation, the inquiry had never got down to the basic causes of the disaster, and had taken the easy course of blaming the accident on hydrogen. Yet there was evidence, even at the time, that such a conclusion was erroneous.

For one thing, the observations of the onlookers, all of whom made detailed depositions to the inquiry, and the behaviour of the fire and the colour of the flames – which were said by all to have been red or orange instead of the almost transparent blue of a hydrogen fire – were inconsistent with the supposed cause of the disaster. NASA scientists re-examined masses of evidence, and the private report of the Zeppelin Company was for the first time analysed and compared with the findings of the US Department of Commerce. Research was also carried out into the results of the inquiries, and experiments devised to test their conclusions.

In this way, new explanations began to emerge to account for the disaster. In the first place, captive hydrogen did not behave in the way that the inquiries had supposed. When vented normally it does not catch fire, even in the presence of considerable voltages of static electricity. But other features of the *Hindenburg*'s structure and operation were brought under suspicion. The fabric which covered the shell and the hydrogen bags had been chemically doped to give it durability and to increase its reflectivity (so that the hydrogen inside would not become overheated and expand), and the separate panels of which this outer cover was constructed were firmly laced together with rope to make them easier to handle. The problems caused by static electricity had been well known by the Zeppelin Company, who believed, with good reason, that any accumulated voltage would be discharged by the lowering of the landing rope on arrival. Unfortunately the dope for coating the airship consisted of powdered aluminium and other compounds including iron oxide – but these were exactly the materials used as solid fuels in the Apollo missions, and, of course, they were highly inflammable. Furthermore, because the covering panels were separate, but laced together, they would discharge separately and would be to a degree insulated from each other by the gap of about an inch between them, since the rope lacing them together, even if wet from rainwater, would not be sufficiently conductive to drain the charge. The smallest of static sparks bridging this gap would be all that was needed to ignite the rocket fuel with which the airship was painted.

The modern researchers concluded, therefore, that the presence of large masses of hydrogen in the airship's bags was quite immaterial in causing the accident, though after the fire started it helped to intensify the flames. It is their view that attention should once again be devoted to the possibilities inherent in the airship as an efficient and economic mode of air transportation.

WHO SANK THE *STRUMA*?

The sinking of the MV Struma *– with its human cargo of nearly 800 Jewish emigrants, including about 100 children – in the Bosphorus Straits in early 1942 created one of the unsolved mysteries of the Second World War. The story of its single survivor cast very little light on the true explanation for the catastrophe, and the cause of the sinking has only recently been made known.*

The *Struma*, a two-masted ship of about 152 feet in length and a beam of nearly 19 feet, was built as a gentleman's yacht at Newcastle in 1867, but was later converted into a river barge for use on the Danube. It finally became a refugee ship in 1940. In 1941, with almost 800 people aboard in the Romanian port of Constanta, the vessel was unsafe and grossly over-loaded. But whatever the danger to the passengers, the chance the vessel offered of emigration was almost certainly preferable to remaining as a Jew in Marshal Antonescu's Romania. He had already shown himself an enthusiastic supporter of Hitler's anti-Semitic policies, deporting and imprisoning Jews and robbing them of their property, while adding a few refinements of his own to the atrocities, such as suffocating people in airtight railway trucks as he shunted them around the country. However, he had allowed this unfortunate batch of about 800 Jews to buy tickets for their passage to Palestine aboard the *Struma*. They were assembled in the port offices at Constanta where they were stripped and systematically deprived of all their valuables. The *Struma* was finally piloted out of Romanian waters on 10 December 1941 and allowed to head south. Within twenty-four hours she reached the Straits, but then her engines failed and she was towed into harbour at Istanbul. There the passengers were to remain, quarantined aboard, for a period of more than two months.

The main cause of their imprisonment was the intransigence of the British and Turkish governments, neither of which was prepared to take any action to resolve their plight or admit any responsibility for it. Britain, the mandatory power responsible for Palestine after 1919, was above all anxious to stay on the right side of the Arabs and consistently refused admission visas to Jewish immigrants. The British were reputed to have done more than this. Throughout the 1940s they were said to have employed MI6 to intercept ships with Jewish refugees aboard in order to prevent them from ever reaching Palestine. The *Exodus*, with 4,500 refugees on board, was turned back in 1946 and forced to return its human cargo to the displaced persons camp in Germany whence they came. In the same year another, the *Pan Crescent*, was intercepted and diverted to British-held Cyprus where its 7,500 refugees were held behind barbed wire until nine months after Israel became independent in 1948. Turkey, officially neutral during the war, had other reasons for keeping its diplomatic nose clean. It was partly that the Turks did not wish to upset Germany, which they would if they flouted the anti-Semitic policies the Nazis favoured; but the Turks had also concluded a trade pact with Germany in the autumn of 1941 under which they agreed to supply the Nazis with much-needed supplies of copper and chromium, both of which were in very short supply in Germany. The Turks, therefore, would do nothing for the refugees stranded in Istanbul.

Without the help of the Jewish community in Istanbul, the passengers would have starved; every day a rowing boat of food supplies left the quayside for the *Struma*, and the community's members did all they could to procure medical assistance for the passengers, who, in their overcrowded conditions, frequently fell ill. Turkish indifference is illustrated by the fact that, even when the British government relented slightly and issued Palestine visas for fifty of the children aboard, the harbour authorities in Istanbul (claiming they had not been informed) refused to allow the passengers to leave the ship. Eventually, however, on 23 February 1942 the *Struma* was towed from the harbour by a tug and allowed to proceed on its journey. The next morning it was torpedoed and sunk, and all except one of those on board perished.

German or Soviet submarines were thought by most people to have perpetrated this outrage. For Germany such an action would have been entirely consistent with the aims of Nazi policies of Jewish extermination. However, there were very few German U-boats in the area of the Black Sea, nor, after the war, did any examination of German navy records show evidence of the sinking. The Soviet Union seemed to be a better bet. Soviet submarines had the opportunity since they controlled the Black Sea with regular patrols; they also had direct orders from Stalin to attack all but Turkish vessels in that area. (In fact when he grew paranoid about Turkey's trade pact with Germany over the export of chromium, Stalin ordered them to attack Turkish vessels too.) Direct proof of Soviet responsibility was lacking, however, until after the end of the Soviet regime. At that time a Latvian ex-serviceman, Ginnordi Kabardin, doing research in the records of the navy ministry, came across a direct report to the effect that Soviet submarine *SH213* had torpedoed and sunk the *Struma* on 24 February at the mouth of the Bosphorus.

A long and fruitless search for the wreck took place in 2000. An English diver, Greg Buxton, whose grandfather had been aboard and had been lost when the ship sank, organised an expedition to the Black Sea to find whatever remained of it. He made exhaustive enquiries among local diving clubs and fishermen until eventually he gleaned some information. The site said by a Turkish diving team to be the last resting place of what they called the 'Jew boat' did in fact contain a wreck at about 100 feet below the surface, but this was a much bigger ship, well over 300 feet in length and 40 feet in beam. It could not possibly be the *Struma*. Two other sites were carefully searched, but these produced nothing. None the less, a memorial service was held in roughly the right area in a vessel chartered for the purpose, and a wreath was thrown into the Black Sea. As yet, however, no one can say with any certainty where the wreck of this tragically unfortunate ship lies.

WHO WAS MR NOBODY?

One of the cleverest and most unscrupulous tricks of the Second World War was the successful deception of the Axis powers by Winston Churchill over the intended landing sites of the Allied armies in the Mediterranean theatre in 1943. As the result of this successful deception, Hitler was convinced that the Anglo-American invasion of southern Europe was scheduled to take place not in Sicily, where the landings occurred in July 1943, but in Sardinia. The difficulties of putting ashore eight fully armoured divisions on a strongly defended enemy coastline, even with air cover and a massive contingent of supporting warships, necessitated the successful achievement of one of the boldest and most imaginative wartime hoaxes in modern times – possibly even since the Greeks pulled off the trick of the Trojan horse.

The hoax involved dumping a human corpse, complete with an officer's uniform and false documents, in the sea off the coast of Spain where it would be washed ashore and plant the idea in the minds of German military intelligence that the intended invasion was planned for Sardinia in the summer of 1943 at points in and around the city of Cagliari on the island's southern coast. Because of this ruse, Hitler was tricked into rushing reinforcements to Sardinia at the expense of the Sicilian garrison, against whose ranks the invasion was really directed.

This story, which was the subject of a best-selling novel and a classic film entitled *The Man Who Never Was*, originated as a top-secret military intelligence plan known as Operation Mincemeat. It was the work of Squadron Leader Charles Cholmondeley, a member of the British Intelligence XX Committee (the letters XX were said to stand for double cross). It was his intention to make the Axis leaders believe that the Allies were planning to strike towards Florence, Naples and Rome in central Italy by the much shorter and more convenient route from eastern Sardinia, rather than the longer way from Sicily via Messina and the whole length of the western coast of the former kingdom of Naples. He conceived the idea of planting misleading intelligence on a recently deceased corpse dumped into the sea in the western Mediterranean disguised as a staff officer whose plane had apparently crashed and left his body floating towards the Spanish coast. The corpse was dressed in full military uniform and a life jacket. In the man's pockets were two love letters from his putative sweetheart, a photograph of her swimming in the Thames at Oxford, and even a letter from his bank manager relating to his overdraft. Securely padlocked to his wrist was a stout leather briefcase containing dossiers of false information regarding the Allies' plans for their invasion of Sardinia, together with fake letters that included similar suggestions. In fact the body had been packed in ice in London, transported by submarine to the Spanish coast near Huelva (where the British knew there was a Nazi secret agent), and there, after a brief burial ceremony, it was dumped into the sea alongside an upturned dinghy. The body was recovered by a Spanish fisherman. He contacted the police authorities who passed the information to the Germans, just as the British intended. The Germans swallowed the bait and the deception worked.

Obviously, for the hoax to be successful, there had to be a body, one that was fairly fresh. Ewen Montagu, the intelligence officer who had responsibility for Operation Mincemeat, located a corpse in one of the refrigerated compartments of the mortuary of a London hospital. The man was then transformed into Captain (Acting Major) William Martin of the Royal Marines, and was furnished with a completely fabricated new identity. After the body was recovered it was handed over to the British vice-consul and buried in a small war cemetery, the Cemetery of Solitude, outside Huelva.

But whose was the body so prepared for this elaborate masquerade? The actual name of the dead man appears on the gravestone in the Huelva cemetery, recorded as 'Glyndwr Michael, served as Major William Martin, RM', but for many years nobody knew who he was. Sixteen years trawling through the masses of records, many of them in the Public Record Office at Kew, ended in 1996 with the discovery of his details in a newly declassified file. Glyndwr Michael, the man whose identity was confirmed in the top-secret file, died in a London hospital in 1943. He turned out to be an illiterate, illegitimate, destitute and feeble-minded vagrant, who spent his time roaming the Welsh valleys and begging from anyone who took pity on him. The failure of any of his relatives to come forward and claim him reinforces the opinion that the secret services never sought their permission to use his body for intelligence purposes, though Ewen Montagu, the man running Operation Mincemeat, maintained in his book on the subject in 1953 that they did. The researchers, on the contrary, have shown that none of the files on Operation Mincemeat contain evidence that Michael's family consented to this use of his body, and no evidence that British intelligence even sought to find them.

Contemporary reports contain a number of references to his death. He seems to have moved from Wales to wartime London and to have fallen on bad times. He took a lethal dose of rat poison, was picked up by the police and taken to hospital where he died. The coroner conducted an inquest on the body, after which it was returned to the hospital mortuary and placed in refrigeration until, apparently without any family permission, it was appropriated by the Intelligence XX Committee. The coroner would have been in a strong position to know whether or not the dead man had relatives, but there was no evidence in his records of the case that his search for them had been a successful one.

Everyone, including Winston Churchill, who used to regale his dinner guests with the story of how he managed to deceive German military intelligence, was immensely proud of Operation Mincemeat and made what may have been exaggerated claims for the importance of its contribution to the Allies' winning of the war. But it must remain an open question whether British intelligence made sufficient efforts, or indeed any efforts at all, to contact Michael's relatives before they employed his body for the deception. Ewen Montagu, who subsequently became a judge, claimed that they did, but this assertion may have been a white lie to justify an otherwise questionable decision.

WHAT WAS GLENN MILLER'S FATE?

The loss of the American dance band leader Glenn Miller in December 1944, in the course of a flight from Britain to France in a light aircraft, was the occasion of one of the most baffling mysteries of the wartime years, the more tragic since he was revered and admired by fellow musicians and many thousands of fans. His disappearance left no trace, and the mystery of his fate remained unsolved for nearly half a century. There were many theories offered to account for it – he had died in Paris when he suffered a heart attack in a French prostitute's bed; he had fallen captive to the Germans who had handed him over to the SS for torture; he had been in a crash and a fire in which he had been badly disfigured and had lost his memory. But none of these theories was ever proved. What is the true story of his end?

Alton Glenn Miller was born in the little town of Clarinda, Iowa, in 1904, son of a schoolmaster, and from his early years he had been mad about music. He left school early during the First World War and worked between the wars in various places as a jobbing musician. He formed his own band in 1937, and by the following year was one of the foremost band leaders in the USA. It was at this time that he perfected the characteristic Glenn Miller sound: he had a large and perfectly balanced brass section, and the main melody line was provided by tenor saxophones playing the same notes as the leading clarinets but an octave lower.

After Pearl Harbor he joined the American forces in 1942, becoming a member of the USAAF. The Air Force ordered him to create a military band, and to this he brought his own distinctive big-band style, bringing the sound to Britain in June 1944. His well-known numbers were now the rage of American and British dance floors.

Servicemen vigorously jitterbugged with the local talent to tunes like 'In the Mood', 'American Patrol' and 'Pennsylvania Six-Five-Thousand', the girls' short skirts flying, or smooched tenderly under the rotating glitter ball to the sentimental rhythm of 'Moonlight Serenade'. When he performed at RAF air bases, Miller did so in hangars with the doors standing wide open so that the music could be heard all over the base.

In December 1944 he agreed that his orchestra should give a Christmas concert in newly liberated Paris for Allied servicemen serving in France. To prepare for this he planned to leave his base at Twinwood Farm, Bedford, in mid-December and fly by light aircraft to the aerodrome at Villacoubley near Paris. He was to be in the company of an American colonel who had to make the journey and who offered him a lift in his little Noorduyn Norseman, a high-winged monoplane with a single radial engine in the nose. His pilot was practised at low-level flights, but all the same the mission was a perilous one: not only was he relying on a simple (and often quite inaccurate) magnetic compass in murky December weather, but the war was still in progress and civil flying was distinctly hazardous. On the day the journey was planned, 13 December, the weather was too bad and continued to be so on the following day; it was only on 15 December that it cleared about midday and the three men took off. They filed no flight plan and hence the details of the journey remained for many years unknown.

Defence installations imposed strict limitations on the route they could have taken: London at this time was a no-fly zone, and there were further severe route restrictions imposed by dense batteries of anti-aircraft guns along the coastline and inland from Norfolk to Hampshire (known as AA gun boxes). Because of the continuing threat to the country from German V1s, these emplacements were under orders to shoot down anything remotely resembling a hostile aircraft. No map of these defences was ever published, and only painstaking research by a modern specialist investigator, Roy Nesbit, has plotted them and enabled Miller's likely route to be discovered. There remained only a narrow corridor between these defences just east of Beachy Head and across the Channel towards Dieppe. This was the route the Norseman took.

At this time, Fred Shaw (like Nesbit, a veteran navigator of the Second World War) was one of the navigators on 149 Squadron, a Lancaster bomber squadron stationed at Methwold, Norfolk, and engaged in night-time raids on Germany while the USAAF carried out costly daytime sorties. He revealed after forty years of silence that he believed the RAF contributed to Miller's untimely death. After being themselves grounded by bad weather on 13 and 14 December, 149 Squadron was ordered on the 15th to take part in a daytime raid on Siegen in Westphalia, about 100 kilometres east of Cologne. The attacking force's 138 Lancasters were each loaded with 4,000lb bombs and hundreds of incendiaries. Delayed until 1130 hours by poor visibility, the squadron eventually took off and headed towards their rendezvous with their fighter escort on the Belgian–German border. The fighters, though, never arrived; they were fogged in at their bases. As a result, the operation was aborted and 149 Squadron was ordered back to base.

The perils, however, of attempting a landing while carrying 4,000lb bombs were well known; the slightest jolt on landing might detonate them and blow the aircraft to smithereens. Hence they were instructed to proceed to the Southern Jettison Zone in the Channel – itself not marked on any chart, but consisting of a circle of 10-mile radius with its centre at 50° 15' N, 0° 15' E. It was here, as the squadron jettisoned its bombs, that Fred Shaw saw far below, through the Perspex blister of his astrodome, the single-engined high-wing monoplane headed for the French coast. One of his fellow airmen also saw it. He called out to his captain to halt the launching of the bombs, but the rain of incendiaries from other aircraft continued and the shock wave from another plane's 4,000-pounder flipped the monoplane over onto its back and it side-slipped into the sea, disappearing without trace.

Sceptics naturally enquired why the incident was not reported at the time, and why Fred Shaw and his colleagues kept quiet about it for so long. The answers to both questions were the same: there were no survivors of the crash; though the type of plane was accurately identified (Shaw had been trained in Manitoba, Canada, where Norsemen commonly flew), no one thought the incident was of much significance; and no one made any link between the accident and the death of Glenn Miller. What was more to the point, 149 Squadron timed the incident at 1342 hours, but Miller had not even taken off from Twinwood until 15 minutes later. It took Roy Nesbit to explain this discrepancy. Everyone had overlooked the fact that the RAF used Greenwich Mean Time (GMT) to time all its missions, but the light aircraft's flight was in the local time, that is in British Summer Time (during the war BST was two hours ahead of GMT in summer, but still one hour ahead even in winter). Thus it seemed perfectly possible for the Lancasters of Bomber Command and the Norseman, if its compass readings were even a few degrees out of true, to have been in the same spot, the Southern Jettison Zone, at the same time, and for the smaller plane literally to have been blown out of the air by the RAF.

Nesbit's explanation for the disaster remained, of course, no more than a theory, and was not put to the test for a number of years. Eventually, in the 1990s, a search-and-salvage plan using sonar and magnetometer readings was implemented in a patch of the Channel measuring 5 miles by 3 in the spot where Shaw observed the accident in 1944. The search area was in a crowded shipping lane and this created considerable difficulties in getting divers into and out of the water before they were run down by passing vessels. Furthermore the Norseman was by now very difficult to locate. Its canvas fabric would have disintegrated within five years, and even its light wooden and aluminium frame would have degraded within ten. After fifty years, nothing would be left except its massive engine block, and this would have become embedded in the gravel floor of the Channel and largely hidden by the growth of marine organisms. A long search was made and there were a number of interesting finds dating from both world wars. Positive identification of Miller's aircraft proved impossible, though one strong contender was a radial engine very similar to the one on the Norseman, though it had eighteen cylinders instead of the nine specified for the aircraft. Nesbit's explanation, therefore, still remains in the realm of theory, but it seems likely that until a novel and superior form of investigation is developed, this is how the story of Glenn Miller must end.

WHATEVER HAPPENED TO THE MISSING H-BOMB?

In the very early hours of the morning on 5 February 1958 a B-47 bomber took off from Homestead Air Force Base, Florida, carrying a 7,600lb Mark 15 Mod 0 thermonuclear bomb containing 4,600lb of conventional explosive, a uranium warhead and a removable nuclear capsule consisting of a plutonium trigger. This bomb was 100 times more powerful than the one the USAAF had dropped on Hiroshima thirteen years earlier; it was capable of obliterating vast areas of eastern America and creating a tidal wave which would be felt as far north as New York.

Not long after take-off, at 3.30 a.m. the bomber suffered a mid-air collision with an F-86 fighter, whose pilot ejected before his aircraft crashed. The bomber crew managed to keep their B-47 in the air, though it had suffered extensive damage and was on fire amidships. The aircraft was directed to land at Hunter Army Airfield outside Savannah, little more than 10 miles away. It reached the runway, but because of mechanical failure was unable to reduce its airspeed sufficiently to make a safe landing. It was therefore ordered to gain more altitude and to jettison its payload at about 7,500 feet in a place where it was not likely to endanger human life, then to return to the base and attempt a landing without its bomb aboard. This it did, dropping its device close to the mouth of the Savannah river in Wassaw Sound off Tybee Beach before landing safely.

This incident created considerable embarrassment in Washington, where the Pentagon wished to avoid public dismay that it had jettisoned a fully armed H-bomb over its own territory. After an initial silence from the US Defense Department lasting several days, the announcement was made that 'a portion of a nuclear weapon' had been released in the area, but that there was no danger to the civilian population since the weapon was 'unarmed'. As things turned out, however, it proved quite impossible to recover the bomb, whether it had been armed or not. The area around Tybee Island was wild and desolate, consisting of swampland, wooded sandbanks and shallow creeks, the configuration of which constantly changed because of the tides. General James Oglethorpe, the Englishman who had founded Savannah, had built a small fort there in 1733, and it was the scene of one of the bloodiest battles in the American War of Independence, when French and American troops used it as a base for their unsuccessful attack on Savannah. In 1958 local newspapers and radio seemed willing, even relieved, to accept the Pentagon's assurance that the H-bomb had not been armed with its nuclear trigger.

Recent research on the incident, however, conducted by Lieutenant-Colonel Derek Duke, a retired USAAF pilot, has cast serious doubt on the Pentagon's truthfulness. The original concern at the dismay which would inevitably result from the announcement that a fully armed H-bomb had been jettisoned over Tybee Island seems natural enough; and the basis for the Pentagon's reluctance to come clean was confirmed in 1966 when another mid-air collision took place, this time at Palomares in the territory of the US's recently acquired NATO ally, Spain. This mishap resulted in the loss of another nuclear bomb for about eighty days and caused great alarm.

Duke has found evidence that the Pentagon was less than truthful in the way it dealt with the Tybee Island incident. Part of this evidence was contained in a Department of Defense document, declassified in 1994, which gave a list of nuclear accidents divided into two categories – 'complete weapons' and 'weapons without a nuclear capsule'. The document clearly put the Tybee Island incident in the former category. Duke's other evidence came from a sworn statement by Howard Nixon, the leader of a loading crew responsible for stowing nuclear devices aboard USAF aircraft at Hunter Base, who declared unequivocally that, though he had been frequently involved in preparing US aircraft for nuclear-armed flights over the Soviet Union, he had never throughout his service loaded 'a nuclear weapon without installing a nuclear capsule in it first'.

The Pentagon, however, is still standing by its original version of events. It has set up a special inquiry commission, and has 'checked and cross-checked' delivery and other records, but still maintains that the Tybee bomb was unarmed, and says that, in any case, the loading crews would have had no idea whether the bomb was armed or not. The Pentagon has further ruled out the possibility of recovering the bomb from the swamps, saying that, since there is no danger of a nuclear explosion, it is better that it stays where it is. Officials further maintain that efforts to raise it from its suspected position on or below the seabed might set off its load of conventional explosives, which would interfere with the water-bearing strata of the area and interrupt or pollute local supplies of drinking water. US government critics in the vicinity of Savannah remain politely sceptical of the government's assurances, but continue to hope that the island, the city, its drinking water supplies and its natural habitat are not blown off the map in a big bang that would end all big bangs.

WHAT SANK THE *KURSK*?

In August 2000 the Russian submarine Kursk *sank in the Barents Sea with the loss of 118 lives. The vessel, supposedly impregnable by reason of her double hull, the inner one 5 centimetres thick, was designed to survive a direct hit, and was divided into nine secure watertight compartments. Nevertheless she was damaged by a suspected explosion in the forward torpedo compartment during an exercise at sea, and hit the seabed 150 metres down. The submarine was powered by nuclear engines, but was not carrying nuclear missiles. Radio communication with the* Kursk *became impossible after the explosion, and repeated rescue efforts by Russian, and later by Norwegian and Royal Navy vessels, were hampered by strong currents and stormy weather in a notoriously difficult area.*

The accident was widely reported in the Western press, which made a good deal of capital out of Russian unwillingness to comment publicly on the disaster and reluctance to allow the Western nations to help in the rescue attempts – a relic of the corrosive secrecy of the Cold War. In the end the Russians said that they were in radio communication with the submarine, which was not true; that at least some of the crew aboard were alive and well, which was not true; that the nuclear reactor had been shut down – but if it had, where were the crew getting their oxygen; and finally that it was all the fault of the USA which had had two submarines in the area, one of which must have collided with the *Kursk*. The Americans responded indignantly by denying that their ships were anywhere near; then by admitting that perhaps they were, but that neither of them had been in a collision; and finally by saying that if the *Kursk* really was impregnable, why were the Russians suggesting that it was a collision that sank her? But it was President Putin who fared the worst in the barrage of criticism. Even the loyal *Komsomolskaya Pravda* demanded answers to its questions: why had he been so reluctant to return from his holidays on the Black Sea; why had he waited four days before taking up

Western offers of help; and why did he hesitate so long
before he went to meet the 600 relatives of the sub-
mariners, before declaring a national day of mourning
and before going to the disaster site to toss a wreath
into the Barents Sea? The whole incident seemed
shrouded in mystery. Is it possible now to find a
solution to the questions that remain?

Beginning on 10 August 2000, the Russian Confeder-
ation staged naval exercises in the Barents Sea area.
About thirty warships, together with the *Kursk*, put to
sea from their northern base at Severomorsk to test
their capabilities and to try out new equipment. On the
first day they tested the artillery and the missiles with
which the surface vessels were provided; on the
second day they were to rehearse their response as
the *Kursk* staged a mock attack on the fleet. At 9 a.m.
the submarine was in routine contact with surface
vessels, but that was the last that they heard from her.
They waited all day, but it was only on Saturday
12 August that they were forced to the conclusion that
something untoward had occurred.

A hurried investigation by divers showed that the
front end of the submarine had been shattered by an
enormous explosion. Various possible reasons for this
were put forward: sabotage and terrorism were considered, and dismissed as unlikely; the suggestion was
made that the *Kursk* had struck a Second World War
mine and had been damaged. All these seemed more
likely to cause a mosquito bite than a devastating blow,
and none could satisfactorily explain the enormous
damage the submarine had suffered. Finally the
Russians came round to their American theory, alleging
that there had been at least one US submarine in the
Barents area monitoring the progress of the exercise,

and that this vessel must have collided with the *Kursk*. Their accusations were later strengthened by under-water photographs which seemed to suggest that the side of the *Kursk* had been sliced open by a glancing contact with another submarine, and by high-altitude photographs taken from a Russian satellite which showed a submarine in a Norwegian port apparently undergoing repairs alongside two US warships. The US authorities denied this was one of their vessels, and qualified this by adding that if it was, it was there for perfectly legitimate purposes, citing a recent urgent request for the transfer to Washington of tapes and other data relating to the sinking of the Russian vessel. There could be no other reason for it to put into any foreign port, they added, since nuclear submarines were entirely self-sufficient and could subsist for months without seeking land-based support. So the argument continued for months between the two governments without any sign of an agreed explanation.

Further light on this conundrum was not forth-coming until well into 2001, and then it came from a most unlikely quarter. Seismologists working at Blacknest Monitoring Station, Berkshire, came up with data the significance of which had at first been overlooked. Their monitors had picked up a massive disturbance in the Barents area at the time of the *Kursk* incident. It was equivalent to an earthquake measuring 4 on the Richter scale. Since earthquakes, volcanoes and explosions each produce characteristic signatures, it was possible to deduce that the origin of this trace was a massive explosion, about the equivalent of that which would have been produced by the simultaneous explosion of the submarine's whole arsenal of tor-pedoes. Precisely 2¼ minutes earlier, however, another much smaller trace, less than 100th the magnitude, was recorded – not a collision, but quite clearly an explosion of some kind.

The explanation put forward related to the engineering design of torpedoes. These are normally powered by a small motor that comes into operation when the torpedo is launched and drives the weapon towards its target. This motor is driven by a small tank of fuel and by oxygen supplied from a bottle which is also carried. A new design tested in 1955 for a torpedo type known as the 'Fancy' operated somewhat differently. It used a chemical known as HTP. This was hydrogen peroxide, a perfectly safe liquid, rather similar to water, which, when it was broken down chemically, generated supplies of oxygen for the torpedo motor. When this new type of torpedo was being loaded experimentally aboard HMS *Sidon*, a British submarine, in Portland harbour in June 1955 it exploded, sinking the submarine in harbour and killing thirteen of the crew. A naval inquiry revealed that HTP was unsatisfactory as a propellant. While in its liquid state it is normally quite innocuous, it reacts chemically with bare copper or brass and breaks down into oxygen and water – or rather, at a high temperature, steam. While so reacting, HTP has the unfortunate consequence of expanding its volume by a factor of 5,000. As a result, if the pipe carrying it is fractured, and if it leaks onto unprotected brass or copper components within a torpedo casing, the casing will be burst open with considerable force and the torpedo head may be triggered. In 1955 a *Sidon* crew member accidentally started the torpedo's motor while it was still in the tube. The motor over-revved because it was not in water, the pipe fractured, and the chemical reaction described took place. As a result of this costly accident, the Royal Navy decided to abandon HTP as a propellant and the 'Fancy' design of torpedo was discontinued. The Russians, however, were not privy either to the report which resulted from this accident, or to the accident itself, and as a consequence of their ignorance were still, until 2000, employing propellants of the HTP type in their torpedoes – without adverse consequences.

Having studied the seismological traces, scientists came to the conclusion that aboard the *Kursk* on 11 August there was some minor jolt or knock in the torpedo room (perhaps because of an underwater collision), or perhaps an accidental firing of a torpedo's motor while it was still in the tube. This triggered a leak in the pipe inside the casing, and caused a chemical reaction between HTP and exposed metal components so that the casing eventually burst under the enormous pressure of steam and oxygen that was built up. This registered its trace at Blacknest monitoring station. There was a totally unexpected fireball in the torpedo room, which the crew fought in vain for 2¼ minutes until the heat caused the simultaneous explosion of all the weapons in the torpedo racks and destroyed the entire bow of the submarine, producing a trace on the monitor more than 100 times the magnitude of the first explosion.

The Russians, however, continued to hanker after their original theory. Senior Russian naval officers were unwilling to endorse the idea that such slipshod practices as starting a torpedo engine while it was still in its tube could ever have happened aboard the pride of the northern fleet. Instead explanations other than a collision with a US submarine were offered. Some

Russian investigators believed that a cruise missile launched from the nuclear-powered cruiser *Peter the Great* accidentally struck the *Kursk* or else detonated sufficiently close to it to destabilise it at periscope depth. Others blamed another warship, the *Admiral Kuznetsov*, whose captain was dismissed only days after the disaster, for ramming the *Kursk* amidships, destroying the bulkhead between the first and second compartments and causing uncontrollable flooding. For this reason retired Vice-Admiral Yevgeni Chernov condemned the Russian Ministry of the Navy's plan to cut off the submarine's bow and only raise the stern of the *Kursk* (in order to recover more than the twelve bodies brought up so far) as an attempt to cover up the real cause of the disaster.

Yet another explanation emerged at the end of October 2001 when the remains of the Russian submarine were eventually salvaged. Russian scientists then revealed for the first time that the accident occurred when the crew were attempting to fire a prototype torpedo capable of travelling 30 kilometres at 160kph. During the launch a gas-generating mechanism jammed, causing an explosion that sent a huge flame into the compartment behind, which held a further twenty-three weapons. Precisely 135 seconds later seven of these exploded, blowing the front of the *Kursk* apart. British scientists observed that this scenario was frighteningly similar to the disaster which overtook the *Sidon* in 1955.

Officially, however, the Russians have not yet abandoned their theory of a collision with a US submarine. Nor do they intend to tell the rest of the world whether they are abandoning their experiments with the new type of torpedo.

6

Mysteries, Secrets and Disappearances

WHAT HAPPENED TO THE FIRST COLONY OF VIRGINIA?

The misfortune that befell the first settlers in Virginia has long perplexed those studying the story of Britain's earliest colony in North America. Of the people who landed at Jamestown in Virginia in the spring of 1607, seventy died within the first few months, and before 1610, in the period known to the settlers as the 'starving time', there was a mortality rate of about 80 per cent. Various theories have been advanced to explain this catastrophe, but the real explanation of who or what was to blame remains a mystery.

The first three vessels of the London Virginia Company – the *Sarah Constant*, the *Godspeed* and the *Discovery*, all under the command of Captain Christopher Newport – carried to the New World about 300 would-be settlers and landed on the James river. Coming chiefly from London and East Anglia, the settlers were a mixed bunch. Some were 'decayed' gentlemen who came to the new settlement in the hope of filling their purses with the gold and silver with which the new country was supposed to abound; some were convicts; but many others were artisans and craftsmen recruited for their usefulness and their willingness to work. Their journey, which began in the autumn of 1606, but which was prolonged to five months on account of dreadful weather, was cramped and dangerous. It was also turbulent. Because they had sailed under sealed orders, no one knew who was to command the settlement; hence there was a good deal of jockeying for position among those who hoped to be named as leader. Captain John Smith, eventually a member of the rather un-wieldy ruling council, himself spent time in detention below decks during the voyage. The long journey also meant that the settlers missed the planting time when they should have been on the land starting the culti-vation of their first crops; hence supplies continued dangerously short in the period after their arrival.

The intention was that the settlers would establish a fort to defend themselves – possibly against the Spaniards, who wished to maintain their monopoly of power in the New World, but certainly against the numerous Indian tribes who might attack them – and go on to trade with the local inhabitants until the colony was self-sufficient in supplies. Unfortunately, the area produced nothing much more than timber and tar, which might in more settled times have been used as items of export or for shipbuilding, but which certainly could not be used for trade with the local Indians. Furthermore, the site which Newport chose, though close to the shoreline, was low lying, swampy and malarial, and lacked fresh spring water for the settlers to drink. There was little movement of the water in the area around the fort, with the result that the settlers, like the inhabitants of London at the time, found themselves drinking from the same water source in which they dumped their sewage.

Smith – later to become the colony's overall commander and to marry Pocahontas, daughter of local
chieftain, Powhatan – headed back to England in the
summer of 1607 to obtain further settlers and more
supplies; but only a matter of days after his departure
the colonists began to suffer. Further efforts to send
assistance to the colony – an expedition in 1609 and
another of nine ships under Sir Thomas Gates in 1610
– did not provide the help required; if anything they
added to the numbers of those afflicted. The new-
comers found the settlement 'in the last stages of
wretchedness', but themselves were soon overtaken by
the same 'profanity and riotousness' and handicapped
by 'such diseased and crazed bodies' as the existing
settlers.

The written records of the settlers are scanty. Most of
them perished within the year in their new sur-
roundings, and for a long time it seemed likely that
they died from a combination of civil conflict,
starvation and sickness. Archaeological records for
many years were non-existent, since the precise site of
the settlement was forgotten and has been only
recently rediscovered. A wealth of original artefacts
began to come to light with the beginning of excava-
tion, but the remains of the first body emerged only a
few years ago.

Civil conflict and starvation. The body discovered was
that of a young man, about twenty years old, who was
one of the original settlers. Scientific testing of his
tooth enamel showed he had been born and brought
up in Cornwall. Was his death an execution, a murder,
or had he been killed as the result of a violent affray,
perhaps produced by a quarrel over the rapidly

dwindling stocks of supplies? Such quarrels were not unknown. The settlers' journals tell even darker stories, for instance of a man who killed his wife, salted her body and then ate it, or of a party which raided an Indian graveyard and dug up a corpse buried shortly before for the purpose of eating it. Settlers' records agree on the desperate shortage of foodstuffs especially in the years 1609–10. They were compelled to eat their domestic animals – hogs, dogs and horses; they were even forced to eat rats and smaller animals normally regarded as vermin. They could not barter with the Indians for food, since it seemed that they, too, were starving. That this was a time of acute starvation is borne out by dendrochronological evidence derived from closely spaced growth rings on the trunks of surviving trees which tells of serious drought in the years 1606–12. Yet the curious fact remains that at Fort Algernon and Point Comfort, only 40 miles downstream of Jamestown, there was no evidence of drought; indeed, the settlers there had enough food for barter with the Indians and even for feeding up their hogs.

Sickness. An alternative explanation of the sufferings endured by the Jamestown settlers is disease. The colonists' records complained of the unhealthiness of the spot chosen for their camp: it was marshy, often covered with a foul miasma or fog, and the water from the creek was slimy, filthy and foul-tasting. Perhaps the victims were too enfeebled by their illnesses to go downstream to get help. Their condition was made worse by the unhealthy air, scant food supplemented by items of diet to which they were unaccustomed, and by their flimsy and leaky housing. Many of them were said to be suffering from what was called at the time the 'bloody flux' – a particularly unpleasant form of dysentery – though there were others whose symptoms seem close to typhoid, which is chiefly spread through impure water. There was nothing new in populations suffering unexplained bouts of incurable plague; indeed, it happened in Europe all the time. Yet the disease was not confined to the hot unhealthy summer months; it seemed to occur even in midwinter when normally it would be expected to decline. Furthermore, it was seen to flare up after the departure for home of the various expeditions' vessels, almost as if it were subject to human planning instead of being truly random.

However, the symptoms displayed by the sufferers were not entirely consistent with either dysentery or typhoid fever. The records suggest that the sick demonstrated a tendency towards unexplained swellings, heavy bruising of the limbs, even to hallucinations, delusions and incipient madness, and to the peeling of the skin (a condition known in the medical texts as exfoliative dermatitis). Such symptoms persuaded Dr Frank Hancock, an eminent American pathologist and himself a native of Virginia, that the natural course of the epidemic was exacerbated by what seemed to him to be clear cases of arsenic poisoning.

Poisoning. Murder by arsenic was by no means uncommon in the sixteenth and seventeenth centuries. It was swift; it was sure; and after the victim's death the poison's presence was not easy for the doctors of the time to detect. It was unlikely to enter significantly into the bones; thus arsenic ingested in the seventeenth century would leave very little trace for the modern

pathologist to go on in surviving skeletons. Furthermore, in the seventeenth century arsenic was readily
available. It was sometimes taken in small doses by
ladies who wished their skin to become fashionably
pale, and it would almost certainly have been carried
aboard ship in the form of ratsbane for the elimination
of vermin. These circumstances gave rise to the
suspicion that the poison was administered by someone operating secretly who wished the Virginia
settlement to fail.

There was a good deal of espionage going on at this
time between Catholic and Protestant countries, and
hence Dr Hancock suspected that the culprit may well
have been either a Spanish spy or an English Catholic
sympathiser.* Examination of the artefacts turned up
in the Jamestown settlement shows the presence in
what was previously supposed to have been a purely
Anglican settlement of a good many Catholic relics.
Rosaries, papal medallions and other Catholic icons
indicate that many of the settlers had Catholic lean-
ings; indeed, one Catholic sympathiser, Captain George
Kendall, was actually shot by his fellows for his
religious beliefs in 1609. In 1605 the Gunpowder Plot
shook England when a group of activists proposed to
blow up James I and the Houses of Parliament in order

* The Spaniards were uncertain of the dangers presented by
  the English colony in an area they claimed as their own, and
  even of its exact location. They sent a succession of spies to
  the area to make further enquiries. In 1609 three of them
  were captured by the English. Subsequently an Englishman
  by the name of Clark was seized and carried off in a Spanish
  caravel. It was only in 1616 that the affair blew over with an
  exchange of the spies for the prisoner.

to further the Catholic cause. During the questioning after his arrest Guy Fawkes had no hesitation in identifying Baron Thomas Arundel as a known Catholic sympathiser and an amateur alchemist. In 1606 Arundel had been the principal advocate of a Catholic colony in North America, and had actually reconnoitred the coast of Maryland with a view to establishing one. His surviving correspondence from this time (with the Spanish ambassador) suggests that he wanted to do something noteworthy for the Catholic faith. At the time of the Virginia expedition, however, he had been shouldered aside and denied permission to sail; he might well have resented his exclusion and may have plotted the ruin of the colony through the use of his poisons.

Much of Hancock's thinking must remain in the realm of speculation, and in any case arsenic poisoning does not explain the whole number of fatalities; but the theory may have some truth in it and would account for features of the tragedy that remain otherwise inexplicable. Whatever its cause, the suffering of the colony continued for ten or twelve more years. It was only after 1625, with the adoption of tobacco cultivation, that Virginia was transformed into a successful trading post, ruled by an iron discipline and with life there hated by most of its people.

WAS DR SAMUEL MUDD A VILLAIN AND A TRAITOR?

For nearly 150 years the name of the doctor who assisted President Lincoln's assassin has been popularly execrated, just as the president's own reputation has been revered. The question of whether Dr Samuel Mudd deserved the harsh verdict passed upon him by a US military court in 1865 only surfaced again at the end of the twentieth century, and now serious efforts are being made to rehabilitate him. Was the verdict pronounced upon him for assisting the murderer while he was in flight anything other than a knee-jerk response to furious Northern indignation at the loss of the much-loved president?

The murder took place on Good Friday 14 April 1865 when President Lincoln attended a performance of *Our American Cousin*, a satirical comedy being presented at Ford's Theatre, Washington. Here Lincoln was shot in the head during the performance by John Wilkes Booth, a half-mad Southern actor, who jumped from the theatre box onto the stage and gabbled an incoherent speech before fleeing. In jumping, he caught his spur in the draperies, fell and broke his shin bone. He rode in considerable pain by horse into Maryland, where he stopped at the door of Dr Samuel Mudd and asked to have his broken leg set. Dr Mudd did not attempt to deny what he had done when questioned by the authorities; he simply said that he did not know and had not recognised the president's assailant. Booth was later cornered and shot dead by Union troops in a barn on a Virginian tobacco farm.

Feelings against those accused of complicity in the murder plot ran so high that Mudd and seven others were brought before a military court and convicted of aiding and abetting the assassin. Four, including a woman, were hanged, and Mudd, who escaped the death penalty by a single vote, was sent to life imprisonment in a jail on an island off the Florida

Keys, where four years later he was pardoned by Lincoln's successor, President Andrew Johnson.

In 1992 Mudd's elderly grandson persuaded the US army review board to set aside the conviction on the grounds that the doctor was a civilian and should never have been indicted before a military court. But President George Bush Snr, and after him President Clinton, both overruled the board and took the view that the jurisdictional issue was resolved at the time of the original trial. In 1998 Richard Mudd, the 97-year-old complainant in the case, continued to pursue the matter, arguing that the conviction had resulted in lasting damage to his family's reputation. He continued to press his belief that his grandfather was 'only a doctor doing his duty to a patient'.

Others, however, have taken the view that Booth sought out Mudd because the doctor was known to have been an opponent of Lincoln, and was indeed reputed to have been involved in an earlier plot to kidnap the president. Whether or not Dr Mudd knew the man he helped, and if he did whether he was aware of the deed Booth had just committed, remains unknown.

THE MYSTERIOUS DISAPPEARANCE OF THE
DUKE OF PORTLAND

One of the most intriguing and baffling mysteries of the nineteenth century occurred in astonishingly normal circumstances in 1898. In that year a very ordinary woman, Annie Druce, made an application to the Bishop of London to dig up her father's body from its grave in Highgate cemetery,

*where it had been buried in 1864. The bishop
passed the request to his legal adviser, Dr T.H.
Tristram QC, and in due course the barrister called
Mrs Druce for an interview. She brought with her a
vast dossier of photographs, copies of documents,
sworn affidavits and the like, all tied up in pink
ribbon, and she told an extraordinary story.*

Her father, Thomas Charles Druce, a humble employee
of the Post Office, was supposed to have died in 1864
and been buried at Highgate; but she contended that he
had not died at all, and that his coffin was weighted
with lead and otherwise empty. Throughout his life he
had suffered from a skin complaint which covered him
with purple patches if he exposed himself frequently
to bright light; it also gave him a bulbous nose, very
obvious from the photographs she produced. By an
odd coincidence the same complaint was suffered by
George Cavendish-Bentinck, 5th Duke of Portland,
who led a life of seclusion at his family seat at
Welbeck Abbey, Nottinghamshire.

When the duke travelled to and from London, he did
so in a coach specially constructed so that he could
not be seen from the outside; his servants and estate
workers were forbidden to acknowledge his presence,
and he spent enormous time and energy in laying out a
labyrinth of chambers and passages beneath his home,
so that for long periods he hardly ever emerged above
ground. For about half the year he was never seen at
all, just as Thomas Druce was never seen for the other
half of the year. It was Annie Druce's contention that
her father and the Duke of Portland were one and the
same person, and she proposed to prove her point by
exhuming the coffin in which he was supposedly

buried. To Dr Tristram this sounded extraordinary, though he acknowledged that her claim to the owner-ship of the Portland family millions was undoubtedly a sufficient reason for her to establish herself as the rightful duchess.

The support of the rest of her family was denied to Mrs Druce, however. In particular her brother Herbert opposed the opening of the family vault and declared his sister a lunatic. In due course the case came up at the consistory court of the Diocese of London. Brother Herbert renewed his opposition to the exhumation, but Annie Druce denied that this was an exhumation, since in her view there was no body in the coffin. She had compiled a dossier of photographs and a careful catalogue of dates to bear out her claim; she had sworn affidavits from twenty-three independent witnesses to corroborate her story; and finally she submitted in evidence her father's death certificate, which did not state the cause of the death and was not signed by any doctor. The court listened attentively to Annie Druce's evidence and rose for two weeks, in order to allow time for anyone objecting to the exhumation to submit a caveat to prevent it. Herbert Druce and his lawyers determined to take this course of action.

Herbert shortly after approached his sister and offered her first £2,000 and later £5,000 to abandon her absurd quest, but she refused. In response to his objections Annie unkindly reminded him that since he had been born before his father's marriage to his mother he was illegitimate and therefore not entitled to an opinion. Later, though Annie could scarcely afford it, she herself took legal advice. She learned that a caveat was simply a delaying document that pre-vented a legal judgment from being executed, but more importantly she learned that her opponents, under cover of this, might use the breathing space to apply for a writ of prohibition under the Burials Act which would permanently prevent exhumation. Her solicitor, though, suggested a different way of tackling the problem: she should apply through the Probate Division for a re-examination of Charles Druce's estate on the grounds that he had not died, so forcing the Court of Probate itself to seek an exhumation in the course of its enquiries.

Herbert Druce and his legal team, however, now secured the transfer of the case from the consistory court to the Queen's Bench Division of the High Court, and Dr Tristram found himself having to defend his earlier decision. An even higher-ranking QC objected to the profanity of digging up a body on such a pre-posterous pretext, and Tristram found himself echoing Mrs Druce's arguments that if there was no body in the grave there could be no profanity in digging it up. The trial judge declared that, in this ambiguous case, the home secretary's permission should be obtained as well. However, the home secretary, when asked, rather perversely declined to grant a licence on the grounds that, if the applicant was right, there was no body in the grave to dig up. The judge, acting on his own initiative, said he had himself no objection to the opening of the tomb and so passed the ball neatly back to its origin, with Dr Tristram.

Before the opening took place, however, there was a new development. In a London evening paper there appeared a report from Australia that back in 1816 Charles Druce had been married to an Elizabeth Crickmer, who though later separated from him had never been divorced. She lived until 1851, and it was only after that date that Druce took a second wife. This had the effect of leaving in no doubt Herbert Druce's illegitimacy, since he had been born four years before his father's marriage to his mother. But what was more germane to the case was that old Mr Druce had produced a son by his first marriage, George Hollamby Druce, who was working as a miner in Australia, and was, if Annie's case was upheld, the rightful Duke of Portland.

When the consistory court reconvened several weeks later the barrister previously appearing for Herbert was now representing George, the Australian Mr Druce. In the teeth of Annie's shrill opposition, George was claiming Charles Druce's entire estate, and now demanded of the bewildered Dr Tristram that he should confirm his father's death by having his tomb opened and the body exhumed. For good measure he declared his intention of bringing a private action against Herbert for perjury for having stated in evidence to the Court of Probate that he had seen his father's dead body before burial. He had taken the precaution of furnishing himself with the necessary funds for any legal action by launching in Australia a Druce-Portland Claimants Co., with a share capital of £30,000.

The second case was heard in Marylebone magistrates' court shortly afterwards. This time the incumbent 6th Duke of Portland, who had inherited the title on the death in 1879 of his eccentric bachelor cousin, was present with two solicitors to hold a watching brief. The lawyer representing George read out the transcript of the deposition made by Herbert, which he averred was totally untrue. The complainant produced two key witnesses: a Mr Caldwell, who had arranged the mock funeral, and a Miss Robinson, who gave evidence that she was Charles's mistress and was well aware that Druce and the Duke of Portland were the same person, and indeed was currently living in a flat in Maida Vale, a property given to her by the duke. He also provided her with an annuity of £240 per year. She clinched her case by producing from around her neck a gold locket in which were displayed photographs of her lover, in both his *personae*. She was in the know about Charles's decision to live the rest of his life as simply the duke and that he had been much amused to go to his own 'funeral', attended by about fifty horse-drawn carriages which Caldwell had filled with retired gentlemen from the Solicitors' Home.

Herbert was now backed into a corner, and felt obliged to agree to George's demand (and Annie's, though she now had less to gain by it) for the exhumation of the body. Accordingly, the vault was opened in the early hours of 31 December 1898. Scaffolding was erected around the plot so as to screen it from the eyes of the inquisitive public, and the site was lit by magnesium flares standing on the surrounding graves. A winch hauled out the coffin, still bearing its engraved nameplate, 'Thomas Charles Druce'. At length the coffin, screwed down and sealed with lead, was opened. Inside lay the shrouded body of Charles Druce, exceptionally well preserved and still recognisable after the passage of thirty-four years.

The discrediting of the testimony of the two witnesses Caldwell and Miss Robinson followed almost immediately, and with it the collapse of George's entire case. The gold locket had suffered amateurish efforts to erase its hallmark, but close police scrutiny showed that in fact it was made not in

1864 but in 1896; closer attention to their testimony revealed that both had been bribed to perjure themselves.

In the end the whole world was satisfied that Charles Druce lay dead and buried in Highgate cemetery. The only person in disagreement was Annie Druce, who was now committed permanently to Lewisham Asylum. She was of the opinion that Charles Druce and the 5th duke were one and the same person, and she had begun compiling a dossier of evidence to use in an attempt to secure the opening of the vaults at Welbeck Abbey, where the duke had been interred in 1879. Her difficulty lay in explaining the question of if Portland/Druce had died and been buried in 1864, who had played the role for the following fifteen years? But nobody listened to her in any case and the duke's grave lies undisturbed to this day.

WHAT IS THE SECRET OF THE DEAD SEA SCROLLS?

In 1947 a shepherd-boy in southern Palestine discovered in a cool, dry cave in the hills above the Dead Sea at Qumran a series of earthenware jars containing fragments of ancient scrolls of documents. When archaeologists examined them they were tremendously excited. Biblical scholars hailed them as the oldest existing copies of the Old Testament and other scriptural texts, dating perhaps from more than 2,000 years ago, and surviving through freak conditions of environment and climate. These scrolls were, however, in an extremely delicate state, and likely to disintegrate into thousands of tiny fragments if efforts were

*made to unroll them. Some had fallen apart
already so that the storage jars were filled with tiny
pieces which had to be fitted together like jigsaw
puzzles. It was believed that the writings originated
in pre-Christian times and were produced and
hidden by Essenes* or by others of the semi-
hermitical communities who lived at that time
around the Dead Sea. The writings were carefully
hidden away before the Romans destroyed
Jerusalem in AD 70. Further discoveries were made
between 1947 and 1956 until over 800 scrolls and
heaps of fragments had been assembled.*

For over forty years a team of eight carefully selected
scholars pored over the scrolls, assembling, trans-
cribing, translating and publishing them. As a result of
these studies new theories were put forward about the
character and teachings of the holy men of the time,
new theories on Christianity were suggested, and
hundreds of amendments were made to the text of the
Bible. Until 1991 the Dead Sea scrolls team kept a tight
grip on their sources, and voices were raised that
hardly anyone outside this small circle had ever seen
them; but in that year the Israel Antiquities Authority,
which controls the scrolls, announced that in future all
scholars should have completely free access to the
photographs which had been made of them. However,

---

* The Essenes were members of a religious sect that existed in
Palestine in the second century before Christ, reputed to be
ascetic in character. A close secrecy developed about the sect,
and its members shunned public life and temple worship,
choosing instead to live as hermits far away from others.

this authority did not suddenly become more co-operative; it left many legitimate enquiries unanswered and restricted access to the scrolls to selected representatives of certain major universities.

Some scholars defended this restrictiveness and objected to free access. Norman Golb, Professor of the Jewish People at the University of Chicago, made the observation, 'There are places where people are qualified to do this work in a civilized society, and they are called universities.' All the same, there are many other scholars who disagree with the findings of those allowed access, or who marvel at what they have missed in forty years of intensive study. The researcher Neil Altman claims that some of the scrolls are sprinkled with instances of Arabic numerals which did not come into use until more than five centuries after they were supposedly written, and that in the Book of Isaiah there has been later inserted a reference to the very un-Jewish expression 'mother of God'. He even claims to have found an insertion of what appears to be a crudely written Chinese character meaning 'God, divine King, deceased King, Emperor'. While completely at a loss to explain this last insertion, Altman claims that the other numerical and similar annotations have a cabbalistic significance, and refer to magical practices originating in Judaism around the fifth century AD. In another scroll called the 'Testimonia', he claims that the word 'Jeshua' does not refer to Joshua as previously thought, but to Jesus's Hebrew name, *Jeshua*. He has also found the insertion of '3x', which he believes is a cabbalistic reference to the Trinity – again quite out of place in the pre-Christian era. In these criticisms Altman is by no means alone.

Another, Peter Pick, formerly Dean of Arts and Sciences at Columbia Pacific University, California, asserts that the inclusion of these letters and numbers indicates a medieval origin for the writings, since it is impossible for them to appear in documents that are supposed to have been compiled up to a thousand years earlier. Whether the annotations are contemporary with the documents is not clear. The mystery is further compounded by the fact that some of them appear to be missing from the first photographs taken of the scrolls.

Elliot Wolfson, Director of Religious Studies at New York University, claims to have seen very similar cabbalistic writings before, in texts dating from the seventeenth century, and believes it is a code used by scribes composing magical writings. He claims to have seen cabbalistic signs such as '3x' in late Christological texts, but declares it is quite impossible to 'have a 3x in a text from Qumran'. Professor Chaim Hames of the Ben Gurion University, Israel, also believes that the mixture of Western letters and numerals with Hebrew script has been seen before and is used as a medieval occultic code. Robert Eisenman, Professor of Middle East Religions at California State University, Long Beach, remains firmly convinced that the scrolls are of the pre-Christian era, but so far has made no suggestions as to how or when these mysterious insertions were made.

Hence it appears that the mystery of the Dead Sea scrolls has been by no means solved, and controversy continues over their true historical and biblical significance: no one can say for certain whether they are genuine; whether, if genuine, they have been tampered with; or whether they are entirely misleading.

WHAT HAPPENED TO SHERGAR?

On the evening of 8 February 1983 a group of armed men wearing masks raided Ballymany Stud Farm, near Newbridge, County Kildare, broke into the house there and threatened the Fitzgerald family, who lived and worked at the stud, with machine-guns. Then they held the wife and the seven youngsters of the family hostage while the husband, Jim Fitzgerald, identified among the numerous resident thoroughbreds in the stables the racehorse Shergar, the Aga Khan's recently retired £10 million horse who had been put to stud on the farm. The raiders led out the horse, loaded him into a box and drove off with both the animal and his groom. Fitzgerald was forced to lie on the floor of one of the three vehicles, his head covered with a coat as the gang drove off. He was released in the early hours of the morning on the dual carriageway leading to Naas, about 7 miles from the stud farm. Later that day the Irish police, the Garda, announced that the horse had been kidnapped, and that the kidnappers, believed to be the IRA, had demanded a £2 million ransom.

Shergar was one of the most successful racehorses of the late twentieth century. Born at the Aga Khan's stud in County Kildare in 1978, by Great Nephew out of Sharmeen, he was put out to train at Newmarket and ridden by jockeys such as Lester Piggott. The jockey who probably knew him best was Walter Swinburn, who rode him to victory in a splendid series of races beginning with the Guardian Classic Trial at Sandown Park in April 1981. Shergar developed from an inexperienced two-year-old into an outstanding three-year-old, winning a series of six brilliant races between 1981 and his disappearance in 1983, including the Chester Vase, the Epsom Derby (twice), the Irish Sweeps Derby and the King George VI & Queen Elizabeth Stakes. His last race was the St Leger at Doncaster in September 1982. He was only ever beaten twice, and earned in total over £320,000 in prize money for his owner. On his retirement from racing at the end of 1982 he was put out to syndication for thirty-three fully paid-up shares, each of £80,000. At stud he sired thirty-five foals, at least one of which was sold for 260,000 guineas.

The newspapers made great publicity from the kidnap. There were all sorts of rumours about Shergar's fate, including a light-hearted cartoon in the London *Standard* that showed a milk float being pulled at 50mph through a southern Irish town by a suspiciously fit dray horse. There was, however, very little progress in the official case. The numerous members of the racing community in the Irish Republic were shocked and frightened: if they gave in and paid the ransom demanded, no stable would be safe from the kidnappers' attentions. Shergar's trainer, Michael Stoute, was appalled by the whole affair. The Aga Khan's manager at the stable, a Frenchman called Ghislain Drion, played his cards so close to his chest that all his answers to questions were utterly cryptic. The police made little progress. The officer in charge of the investigation, Detective Superintendent James Murphy, was capable and experienced, but he found himself presented in the unsympathetic British press as a rural hayseed, a kind of Irish Inspector Clouseau. He was up against a stone wall of silence, and could make little headway with the case.

The whole inquiry into the missing horse resembled nothing so much as an expensively staged drama with a supporting cast of thousands but no leading man and no script. It seemed as though each participant had his own private agenda and was determined to tell no one else of it. Perhaps the chief player should have been the Aga Khan himself, but he never came anywhere near Ireland during the whole investigation, and his pronouncements were always gnomic and distant, perhaps in keeping with his semi-divine status. Other senior figures in the hierarchy, like Ghislain Drion, seemed disinclined to take any sort of action without his approval, and avoided taking responsibility for any decision. They wanted to have nothing to do with the police. Instead Drion preferred to surround himself by his own private militia of retired SAS officers. The numerous – and often well-connected – members of the owning syndicate held all sorts of conflicting opinions about whether the full ransom should be paid, whether sums short of ransom should be offered as a reward for information leading to the horse's recovery, and if so whether £50,000 or £150,000 would be an appropriate figure to put up. Various insuring bodies connected with the racing industry, including Lloyd's, while definitely opposed to paying the full ransom, suggested a number of different sums as a reward. Secret feelers were put out, either by the kidnappers themselves or by other persons in the know who were prepared to sell information, suggesting a higher level of reward, one of their number making a series of anonymous phone calls to an investigative reporter called Colin Turner, who eventually wrote a book on the subject (*In Search of Shergar*, Sidgwick & Jackson, 1984). Perhaps unsurprisingly, the whole inquiry, though it dragged on until the early months of 1984, proved quite fruitless.

Not even the most obvious of the questions asked ever received an answer:

Who was responsible for the kidnap? The most commonly offered answer was the IRA, yet they were never implicated in the affair and, unusually, never claimed responsibility for kidnapping Shergar. The theory was put forward – but never satisfactorily proven – that the IRA were merely the front men for a much bigger deal with an international body, perhaps with Arab or Middle Eastern connections, which was offering them arms or money in their war in the North as the price of their silence.

Why was Shergar never seen again, and why did the demands for his ransom end so soon after his disappearance? It was suggested that perhaps the horse had been injured during the kidnap and had had to be shot, or that those who abducted him did not know enough about horses and lacked the skill or the facilities to keep him alive. Yet telephone calls continued to assert that he was alive and healthy until well into the autumn of 1983.

Was the demand for a ransom perhaps no more than a blind? Was the kidnap not for ransom, but for revenge by someone with a grudge against the Aga Khan? There were a number of individuals in the racing community, wealthy people both inside Ireland and abroad, who seemed to be obvious candidates; and there were other groups with quite different motives. The Aga Khan had crossed swords on purely ideological grounds with the Libyan leader Colonel Gaddafi, who might now be seeking revenge for purely political reasons. Or perhaps the kidnap sprang from religious resentment from some fundamentalist group since the Aga Khan was leader of about 12 million Muslims. At the same time it must be said that if this was a coup directed against the Aga Khan himself – for whatever reason – it seems odd that it was not timed to take place until after the horse had retired and had been put out to syndication.

Had Shergar been spirited out of the Republic by the kidnap gang? He could not be traced in Ulster, and though detailed enquiries were made into the export traffic in horseflesh out of Waterford and the smaller adjacent ports along the south coast such as Dunmore East, they produced a wealth of rumour but nothing in the way of more precise results.

Why did the government of the Republic, which generally had a good record in handling kidnap situations, not play a more active role in the affair? Although the horse-racing industry was worth over £100 million to the country annually, the government played no active role, and within weeks of the kidnap cut back its team of forty detectives on the case to a mere handful. Then on grounds of financial stringency it cut back its enquiries further, even refusing to pay for the heating or lighting of the caravan that was used as an incident room at the stud.

In the end the only people who seemed to wish to continue the case were the newspapers themselves, and in time even they got tired of the stonewalling and the negativity they encountered. After a year or two the inference that Shergar was dead seemed quite inescapable. The only people who evinced the slightest regret were not the owning syndicate, nor the Aga Khan himself, who scarcely noticed it, but ordinary racing enthusiasts who were no longer able to enjoy the sight of this beautiful animal in action.

HOW DOES SPONTANEOUS HUMAN COMBUSTION OCCUR?

The idea of spontaneous human combustion has a well-established place in fiction. Most people know the story told in suggestive detail in Charles Dickens's Bleak House *of the sudden and macabre demise of the sinister Krook, discovered incinerated in his lodgings by two other characters, Mr Guppy and Tony Weevle; they are perhaps less familiar with earlier stories on the same fictional theme written by George Marryat, Nikolai Gogol and Herman Melville. Factual accounts of spontaneous combustion have also appeared many times, perhaps the earliest occurring in 1613 when the phenomenon struck an Italian countess called Cornelia Bandi who mysteriously burned to death in her bedchamber in Verona. A dossier of well over 100 such cases has been compiled in which the same curious story is retold in different situations.*

One of the best documented modern cases occurred in the kitchen of a flat in a baker's shop in Folkestone town centre, Kent, in 1987. The body of a 44-year-old man, Barry Soudain, was found burned to ashes, only his lower legs and his feet remaining. The room was heavily smoke-logged and covered with a yellow grease that turned out to be human fat; yet other materials in the kitchen, even those made out of textiles and plastic, were barely damaged, and there was little fire damage in the vicinity of the body. A kettle half full of water was on the lighted gas-ring nearby, which suggested that the death must have occurred only shortly before the discovery was made. The inquest on the victim reached an open verdict, declaring that he was alive but had a high blood-alcohol level at the time of the fire, and that this may have contributed to the death. The affair caused lively public interest at the time and was the subject of a TV transmission in a BBC science series in 1989 entitled *QED*.

This programme provoked mixed reactions from the people who took part in it. Members of the public and at least one police officer agreed that the BBC producer and her team had used their dramatic licence to give a highly misleading view of the case, as if determined to disprove the possibility of spontaneous human combustion, using phrases in the commentary such as, 'Even in the most bizarre cases there is no need to resort to the supernatural; science can provide a perfectly rational explanation for such deaths.' In fact, no such rational explanation was forthcoming, and those attending the scene were totally dumbstruck by their horrific experience. The programme's suggested explanations for the burning were totally unfeasible: that the gas stove or the electric fire were the sources of ignition – but the fire was switched off and the gas stove was on the other side of the room and was apparently unconnected with the fire; that the victim was set on fire by the gas-ring – but this too was a little far fetched and in any case there was a kettle of boiling water on it undisturbed at the time; that the victim was drunk, or had suffered a heart attack – but he did not suffer from a heart condition, and, though he drank regularly, he did not do so excessively, nor was there any evidence, despite his raised blood-alcohol level, to suggest he had been drinking on this occasion.

The most remarkable feature of the death remained unexplained by the film: though the fire had generated tremendous heat – enough to reduce much of the body to ashes – it had remained inexplicably localised. Only the feet and lower legs remained intact, but curtains and a pile of newspapers, though affected by smoke, were not burned, a polythene dustpan and brush nearby were undamaged, and the ceiling, made of polystyrene tiles, remained untouched. One possible explanation was that, his clothing having caught alight at the gas stove, the victim lost consciousness, fell to the floor and burned from the top downwards like a candle with the wick on the outside. This explanation was never satisfactory since the high temperatures that had been reached could not be accounted for. It was suggested, somewhat improbably, that the body might have reached this state from smouldering for hours; but this kind of fire would not have generated enough heat, and in any case the half-full kettle implied that the death must have been very recent or otherwise it would have boiled dry.

The true number of such deaths tends to be under-reported. The barriers to a fully truthful account of the extent of the phenomenon partly relate to the desire of those who discover the burning to spare the feelings of relatives, but chiefly to the horror and bewilderment of the investigators. Though individual firemen at the scene may confess their bafflement, senior officers may simply say that the cause of the fire is unknown, while investigating police officers look for an ascertainable cause rather than confess ignorance. People in such a situation fear the ridicule of their fellows if they put forward spontaneous combustion as an explanation. Some officials think it will mark them down as a crank, or may even stand in the way of their later promotion. Furthermore, even the wick effect mentioned above is not clearly scientifically established. No one has managed to replicate it in a controlled experiment. Crematorium employees are generally agreed that for a body to be totally consumed by fire, temperatures in the vicinity of 1,000°C are required, and for the bones themselves to be consumed, even higher. In a domestic fire, on the other hand, temperatures seldom exceed 500–600°C. Besides, the main clear difference between ordinary cases of burning and spontaneous combustion is that in the latter the fire springs from within the victim and the body mass itself provides the fuel, while the external application of heat to a body invariably produces blackening or charring but never complete destruction. Normal combustion proceeds inwards, destroying the extremities first and usually failing to reach the internal organs; but in the case of spontaneous combustion it moves outwards, so that the extremities, like the hands and feet and sometimes the head, are left untouched, while the bulk of the torso and the internal organs are entirely destroyed. In this way, a case of spontaneous combustion is visually quite unmistakable, producing fine ash and calcined or powdered bones, with internal organs such as the heart and stomach entirely consumed. In spite of the fact that the human body is 80 per cent water, spontaneous combustion can proceed without the use of any fuel or accelerants. The body does not in fact burn more readily because of the victim's alcohol intake, since alcohol loses its flammability after ingestion; nor can the blame be scientifically put on medicines or the application of creams or other cosmetic materials to the surface, which make no more than a negligible contribution to the conflagration.

So, if scientific explanations of these instances of combustion are lacking, what may be said to be the real cause? A collection of postulated causes is advanced here, these suggestions varying from the ludicrous to the supernatural.

Some prefer a *chemical* explanation: that the materials eaten or drunk by the victim have generated inflammable gases within the body, such as phosphine or methane – it has even been suggested that clothing may have been ignited by the phenomenon of the 'phosphinic fart'! But of course the quantities of these combustible gases would need to be gigantic to create such infernos, and having been generated they would still need somehow to be ignited.

Others have preferred the *electrical* explanation, and have associated apparently spontaneous combustion with massive build-ups of static electricity. A similar explanation is sometimes suggested for the high incidence of diseases such as cancer in those living under, or near, power lines. A link is suggested here by reason of the occurrence of illness in proximity to electricity, especially since some of those killed by spontaneous combustion have previously complained of feeling unwell, heavy or lethargic. However, neither static electricity nor active electrical discharges like fireballs have been shown to reach a sufficient voltage.

Only lightning strikes could have done this, and spontaneous combustion is not especially associated with thunder storms.

The most fanciful explanations are not really explanations at all since they involve the intervention of *supernatural* forces such as ley lines or extra-terrestrial influences, UFOs or even *kundalini* fire (in accordance with the ritual teachings of Hinduism). The application of these cannot, of course, be disproved; but they cannot be proved either within the parameters of existing scientific knowledge.

It seems appropriate to say that, in the light of the large numbers of incidents, there must be a scientific explanation for spontaneous human combustion, but that at our present state of scientific discovery we do not know what it is.

Further Reading

Readers may like to consult the following texts which have been used in the compilation of this book:

Fraser, Antonia, *Mary Queen of Scots* (Weidenfeld & Nicolson, 1969)

——, *The Gunpowder Plot* (Weidenfeld & Nicolson, 1996)

——, *Marie Antoinette* (Weidenfeld & Nicolson, 2002)

Gardiner, R., and Van der Vat, Dan, *The Riddle of the Titanic* (Weidenfeld & Nicolson, 1995)

Hastings, Sir Patrick, *Cases in Court* (Heinemann, 1949)

Hatton, Ragnhild, *George I, Elector and King* (Thames & Hudson, 1978)

Kendall, Paul Murray, *Richard III* (Allen & Unwin, 1955)

Langford, Paul, *England, 1727–1783* (OUP, 1989)

Ludwig, Emil, *Napoleon* (Allen & Unwin, 1927)

Macdonald, Roger, *The Man in the Iron Mask* (Constable, 2003)

Nesbit, Roy C., *Missing Believed Killed* (Sutton, 2002)

O'Farroll, Gerald, *The Tutankamun Deception: the True Story of the Mummy's Curse* (Sidgwick & Jackson, 2001)

Patterson, Richard, *Butch Cassidy: a Biography* (University of Nebraska Press, 1999)

Radszinsky, Edvard, *Rasputin, the Last Word* (Weidenfeld & Nicolson, 2000)

Routledge, Paul, *Public Servant, Private Agent: the Elusive Life and Violent Death of Airey Neave* (Fourth Estate, HarperCollins, 2002)

Shanks, Hershel, *The Mystery and Meaning of the Dead Sea Scrolls* (Random House, 1998)

Tey, Josephine, *The Daughter of Time* (Peter Davies, 1951,
    reprinted by Penguin, 1981)
Tillyard, Stella, *Aristocrats* (Chatto & Windus, 1994)
Trow, M.J., and Trow, Taliesin, *Who Killed Kit Marlowe?
    A Contract to Murder in Elizabethan England* (Sutton, 2001)
Tulard, Jean, *Napoleon* (Methuen, 1984)
Turner, Colin, *In Search of Shergar* (Sidgwick & Jackson, 1984)
Uncovered Editions, *The Saint Valentine's Day Massacre, 1929*
    (London Stationery Office, 2001)
Watson, J. Steven, *The Reign of George III, 1760–1815* (OUP,
    1960)
Weir, Alison, *The Princes in the Tower* (Pimlico, 1992)
Williams, Basil, *The Whig Supremacy, 1714–1760* (OUP, 1962)
Williamson, Hugh Ross, *Who Was the Man in the Iron Mask?*
    (republished in Penguin, 2002)

Index

Entries highlighted in **bold** refer to topics which have separate listing in the table of contents.